Memoirs of a Mad Redneck

Zac Henson

Memoirs of a Mad Redneck

This edition © 2019 Guillotine Press
ISBN: 9781095302576

Library of Congress Cataloging-in-Publication Data
Published in the United States of America

"The man stood at the edge of the plateau. Though he was divided and multiplied on this plane, the transition to the next plane was imminent. He could see behind him a vast wasteland of destruction, with the seeds of some new world beginning to sprout. While this man didn't plant the seeds, he did prepare the soil with the detritus of the old world.

Now he must become something different, a new being entirely. What it will be is unclear, as always, which is how he likes it. He steps off the precipice, into the unknown, with the false hope that the next transformation will be utopia, knowing all along that the transformation itself is utopia. Embrace the madness. Swing on the spiral. Love fearlessly." - Unknown

PROLOGUE

We must all become singularities, of infinite value. The story I'm about to tell is one of a mad, redneck, white, male, auto mechanic, plant worker, husband (twice), uncle, son, grandson, banjo player, singer, drug user, hippie, alcoholic, Christian, agnostic, scholar, organizer, small business owner, and a million other unnameable things. Even this description is overly reductionistic since it is only a manner of speaking and the redneck of yesterday or the last minute is not the one of the present or the future. The pace of change quickens as I approach singularity, the result of which is unbridled creativity, ecstasy, and love.

I have suffered, bled, died, and been reborn numerous times. I have experienced a moment of collective movement where true, singular change was possible and I have watched it dissolve as quickly as it arose in a destructive cauldron of egos and jealousy. I have experienced the doldrums of poverty and grinding oppression of the boss. I have felt the warmth of the body of the one I love and the despair of that warmth used against me. I have succeeded and failed, the latter more than the former, and I have learned important lessons from each. Above all, in my 37 years, I have learned that the only thing necessary is fearless love. Because we will all die, and in terms of geologic time, we die almost instantaneously after we are born, there is nothing to fear, since the worst thing that could possibly happen is death and it is inevitable. Be everything that exists. Experience every perspective. Do not fear, and love unconditionally. Be a singularity.

CHILD

I was born in Birmingham in 1978, 15 years after the Civil Rights Movement, and one year before Birmingham elected its first black mayor, Richard Arrington. I don't remember much until I was five, but I'm told that we spent some years in North Carolina, where my brother, David, was born. My first memories are from Fairfield and most of those memories are sense impressions and not actual events. With current eyes, I can look back and see that Fairfield was transition from a mixed steel city to a predominantly black, poor city, a process created by the combination of white flight and deindustrialization.

I had many black friends as a child and, initially, the racial difference didn't mean much. Our friends played Star Wars together and David always wanted to be Han Solo and, I, Luke Skywalker. Like many children of the eighties, Star Wars had a profound effect on the way I perceived and thought about the world. The epic struggle between good and evil and the belief that patience and persistence wins out for the good stuck. The cavalier approach to fighting the powerful bled into my later activism and produced more than a little consternation among more "serious" activists and organizers.

I was first taught to understand racial cues through Star Wars. My mother, a reformed hippie and fundamentalist stay-at-home mom encouraged the interest in Star Wars, presumably because the clear lines between good and evil fit with our fundamentalist Christianity in the Church of Christ. My mother would often parrot the language of black friends, whose name I no longer remember, by saying "Sta Was," mimicking the Black American English of my friends. Subtlety, she was telling me that I was not like them, she was programming me with the racial roles that she was programmed with from birth. This is how the cycle repeats and the lessons are taught to both blacks and whites from an early age - you are different, and on this culture, this subtle instruction to small children, rests all the powerful institutions of the South and the Birmingham region. Nobody talks about race in Birmingham except to repeat the platitudes that ensure that we never deal with it. People remain poor, some blacks get virtually meaningless positions, and transnational corporations pocket our wealth.

Race in Birmingham is like everybody's crazy uncle Elmore. He does irrational things, he harms everyone, but no one talks about it because it's easier just to pretend that he doesn't exist than to actually face it. There's no shortage of cowardice among the well-connected in Birmingham. Since only 21% of Birmingham's people actually vote in municipal elections, a testament to profound mistrust of governing institutions, local leaders are incentivized to play to older, land-owning, but marginally financially stable residents, while ignoring the plain-as-day issues within the city. Birmingham is and has been in a situation of profound economic crisis for over a decade and probably a lot longer in which the governing institutions don't respond to the needs of the people and the people lose faith in those institutions in a self-reinforcing downward spiral. This is really about class, but race is the tool the powerful use to make sure that we never talk about it. I learned what most of white Birmingham learned which is "they (black people) have their own leadership, why can't they do for themselves," which is a mantra repeated by black and white people alike and serves to obfuscate who is actually in control - global corporations. But, to the people of Birmingham, in all our provinciality and hot, sleepy Southern townness nothing exists outside the boundaries of Birmingham; Walker County to the North and Shelby to the South tops.

We all learn this. We learn that outsiders are to be feared. We learn that race is about tribal solidarity, and the powerful use all this to ensure that we never see the truth - that there is a global attack on our city made by Goldman Sachs and Wells Fargo and their likes. We'll talk incessantly about the sins of disgraced former Mayor, Larry Langford, but we'll never talk about the banks who funded the sewer system, manipulated Langford into signing away our inheritance, and walked away with a few billion and no jail time. Langford was just the black patsy, an easy mark for a desperate city and who took almost 100% of the brunt of the, at this point, well-known strategy of austerity. Get them in debt, charge more, privatize. We haven't gotten to the privatization strategy yet, but I can guarantee you that it's coming. Yet, I learned that everything is tribal and can be explained on the basis of a Manichean struggle between these fictional races.

We're played. We're played off each other to make sure that the money keeps flowing into the coffers. It starts with the enculturation process, the education in family and education.

The miseducation of the redneck included more than just subtle white supremacy; it included a materialistic worldview that measures success by the balance line of the bank account. Being taught this perspective by my parents is understandable. We were poor, poorer than most but not as poor as many. Though both of my parents were college educated, they struggled to put food on the table, but my brother and I probably didn't realize this until much later in life. We looked forward to the biweekly choice of a Star Wars figure, many of which we still own. These little luxuries, going to movies, toys, attending the occasional Auburn football game, going to the zoo and the Museum of Art, shielded us from understanding ourselves as poor and probably was accomplished at great cost by my parents.

Of course, the rugged individualism of my upbringing is raced as well. In the inversion of it, people who don't succeed are solely responsible for their lack of success. It's evidence of their lack of work ethic, of their graft and trifling and backed by a Protestant individualism laced into most of the black community and all of the white community, however inexact those abstractions are. The black bourgeoisie, however tiny, constantly harps on the entrepreneurship of poor people, and, though it's mixed with a genuine care for the race, what is called "respectability politics" is prevalent and pervasive embedded in the "do-for-self" Booker T. Washington work culture that serves the purpose of further demeaning those who've been failed by this culture, white supremacy, capitalism, and, most importantly, the South itself. Whenever anyone speaks out, however imperfect, the black bourgeoisie rushes to tell them to shut up and that "they are trying, but it's more complicated than you understand." It is not complicated at all. The white bourgeoisie control everything in Birmingham and they are fucking all of us, and, while it may be complicated to ingratiate yourself to them and get their resources to help poor communities, the problem itself is not complicated at all. The white bourgeoisie, the people of the suburbs, the people who control all the major social and economic institutions, the people "Over the Mountain" as they are known colloquially, are fucking us. Simple.

Everything that I ever learned, my redneck education was designed to hide this fact. Seemingly innocuous, everyday interactions reinforced the purposely constructed division, the diversionary tactic of race, which not only pits the white working class against the black working class, but the, not necessarily sellout, black bourgeoisie from the black working class.

My class education was all about this diversionary tactic. I was enamored with neoconfederate ideology, an interest spawned by me and my brother's fandom of the Dukes of Hazzard. Encouraged by my parents, I studied Robert E. Lee, Stonewall Jackson, and the Confederate Battle Flag, symbolizing the so-called War of Northern Aggression. Being the nerd that I was, I learned all the arguments as to why the Civil War was not about slavery. I was and am immensely proud of being a Southerner, though, my reasons for being proud now are more "in spite of" instead of "because of," as they were as a child.

The South will never stop fighting the Civil War, which was based on the greatest diversionary tactic ever perpetuated on the working class - that white workers were/are superior to black workers. A grad school colleague, Liviu Montescu, told me that we will never quit fighting the Civil War because it's the only war on our soil in American history, which isn't exactly correct, but I get his point. In Europe there are centuries, maybe even a millennia of wanton murder and ridiculousness over diversionary tactics that are really about territory.

The tactics used to quell unrest throughout the history of the South, and probably throughout the world, are virtually the same. Get oppressed to fight each other. Also simple.

To say that I learned nothing positive from my childhood and adolescent love of the Confederacy would be incorrect. The immense hatred and suspicion of the state that I learned, for the wrong reasons, would stick with me all my life. One of the biggest contradictions in redneck culture is the fervent belief of the oppression of the state, at least the federal state, paired with, what is mostly theoretical, white supremacy and misogyny. I say theoretical because all of my redneck friends have some black friends, who are "good blacks." Blacks and whites work together, but not honestly. They share the shop floor, but they never share how they really feel about the other, and they never attend social events or vote together. The workplace is nominally integrated, but honest dialogue is a chimera. It turns out that most of the black people that rednecks know are stand up people and the welfare mooch black person is more or less a fantasy driving redneck politics.

Southerners, black, white, and indifferent, hate the government. This is the exploit, the bug in the system, the moment of clarity and agreement, that, if used correctly, could lead to profound transformation of the region. The problem is that both sides think that "their" political leaders are defending their interests, while the problem lies with the "other's" political leaders. Joe Reed, Mugabe-like leader of the Alabama Democrats, is a hero to his black constituents and hated by whites, while idiot-despot Roy Moore, elected Chief Justice of the Alabama Supreme Court, is defending white constituents against queers and big government. Race is the perfect tool of the despot.

My father was always involved in get rich quick, multi-level marketing schemes. He was in Ronald White's words a "temporarily embarrassed millionaire," and, as a part time Church of Christ preacher, and pretty good one at that, his rigid and dogmatic Protestant religion supported the belief that hard work leads to success, regardless of how true that actually is. He was a brutal parent, and while I don't remember the brutality specifically, I know that it happened and I know that I lived my childhood in fear of his wrath. I don't blame him; I blame Southern culture in which brutality is how lessons are taught. I call him "Hal." My mother, India, was complicit.

I don't blame my father and mother. They're subject to the same thick, oppressive Southern culture, a culture full of self-defeating and self-oppressive tricks that make our Third World despots' leadership viable. The only respite from the repressive heat of Southern culture is crisp Saturday mornings in October, when Southerners, black and white, suspend the rules of engagement and joyously gather to watch our beloved football, for some, including myself, a quasi-religion. I should say that football is liberatory for all those that don't play it since my state and the South consume the destruction of black bodies as a part of this ritual. It's literally cannibalism and at the same time, it contains the promise of riches, or at least education, for many of these black youth who would otherwise be stuck in situations that are not unlike the above referenced Third World.

One of my first memories was "Bo Over the Top;' a simple play in the legendary mid 80s Auburn teams, in which, Bo Jackson, a consummate legend in Alabama, dove over the top of the scrum into the end zone for a touchdown. My brother and I played football in the front yard. I was Bo and he was Lionel "Little Train" James. We both had the jerseys. In a testament to the complexity of race, and yet, its simplicity, we were taught to respect black people as long as they were in their appropriate place - sports, some entertainment (not hip hop, that's gangster), acting, etc. I can't think of another person that I admired other than Bo Jackson.

Bo Jackson is from Bessemer, Alabama, where my Jewish grandfather on my mother's side had a successful business. Bo has a sort of Paul Bunyan status around these parts. There are stories of him jumping over a Volkswagen and performing other super-human feats. He played both baseball and football and could have been in the Hall of Fame in both sports had he not gotten injured playing football for Los Angeles Raiders, which goes back to the consumption of black bodies and sports,

In some respects, Hal is remarkably successful. His mother was a sharecropper and his father was a low level worker at US Steel. I suspect that his rage at me, a precocious child, had much to do with the brutality of his childhood, but I do not know this for a fact. He was the first in his family to graduate from college with a degree in rural sociology, which is the discipline of my academic mentor at Auburn, Conner Bailey. Hal worked remarkably hard, and though he didn't do so as anonymously as his culture would have suggested, he put food on the table.

When I was six and we were living in Pea Ridge, a rural township outside Montevallo, I had my IQ tested. I'm not sure what precipitated this. I guess people knew that I was "advanced," whatever that means, but I scored off the charts. My teachers began treating me like some sort of alien and my parents clearly thought that this was a pathway to sure wealth and began talking to me about college and careers. At 6.

I was immediately put in gifted classes and my academic environment completely changed. I was special, unique, profoundly talented. I have my doubts about IQ tests. They aren't consistent across race, class, and gender and I don't believe that intelligence can be measured. Anyone who was put in the environment that I was out in as a child would grow to be intelligent and, in many respects, I wonder, looking back on my life, if I ever had any choice in whether or not to be "gifted." My childhood basically disappeared. My disdain for authority began here. I was surrounded by "authority figures" from parents, to teachers, to school administrators who saw me as "potential," not as a living, breathing human being who might want a life starkly different from the one planned for me. At six.

My self-worth became wrapped up in my intelligence. I wore Einstein shirts and studied science relentlessly. Everyone knew that I was going to be a star. This is a mind-fuck for a six year old. No one around me, including myself, understood what intelligence really meant. It was like intelligence was somehow linear, like it led directly to a destination, when, in fact, people who have been profoundly gifted throughout history have had difficult and trying lives. While I don't know if my life has been trying or difficult, it has been different and certainly different from my redneck peers. I never reached the pinnacle of my father's dreams - some whiz financial trader making millions with a keystroke. I never reached the pinnacle of anything, but a life of constant reinvention and exploration of who I am and who I can be. Maybe, that is genius, but it doesn't translate to fame and glory, instead a constant struggle to fit in a world not built for me/us.

We moved around a lot for the next few years, even spending some time in Florida, where my parents almost got divorced and probably would have if not for fundamentalist religion. I vaguely remember living in a "high crime" area and down the street from my elementary school. I was still in "gifted" classes and when we moved back to metro Birmingham, I was told by my "gifted" teachers that smart people weren't supposed to be athletic. That was my last moment in "gifted" classes because as working class people, we valued athletics as much as academics if not more so.

When I was in sixth grade, my father bought my mom a ring that symbolized our move from poverty and the working class. Hal got a job at Halsey Grocery Company, a reputable grocery distributor in Madison, Alabama and we moved into the smallest house in a subdivision in a community transitioning from farming to suburbia. During the move, the ring was stolen and my parents subsequently sued, which almost destroyed the marriage. Twenty years later they would find the ring in Birmingham at a jewelry store.

The incident with "the ring," as it became known in family lore and faintly and seemingly referring to evil and Mordor, was a watershed moment in my childhood. The movers who stole the ring were black and the anger about its loss and the loss of what it represented transformed the respectable racism of the petit bourgeois into the overt racism of rednecks. Thus, when we became petit bourgeois our culture became more working class. Maybe, we were

just honest. [*interesting: lawsuit as symbol.*]

I got involved in my parents' fight over the lawsuit over the movers

and "the ring." Owing to my precociousness, I thought that I could

solve the problem. The problem manifested as money as it always

did in our family, but it was more about values. The lawsuit was

stressing Hal out and my mom wanted to pursue it, not because of

the money, but because of what it represented. It represented my

father's love for her, their struggle, and their success and to give up

on at least compensation for that important symbol seemed like

somehow denying their struggle and accomplishment. I told Hal this

in so many words and it seemed to quell the argument. We

eventually won the lawsuit, but I got the distinct feeling that my

parents were just glad that it was over. I learned from this that my

parents ran all their values through the dollar sign and would soon

adopt this point-of-view myself. I excelled at school. This meant a

lot of money.

　　The culture of our home was highly charged and highly

competitive. School and family had inculcated a type of toxic

masculinity in my brother and I that only being the best counts for anything. My brother and I fought constantly and I was beginning to challenge the authority of my parents and teachers. We were taught to quash our feelings, to be men, to control and dominate, and to not allow anyone to control and dominate us. I lived my childhood under a constant state of siege, which is the self-fulfilling prophecy of Southern culture - that the world was hard and required hard men, thus, parents and other institutions must make the world hard to prepare hard men for the hard world. Explains the love of football, which is nothing if not hard. I was 13.

In the midst of this was probably my favorite memory of my father. Our summer league baseball team's coach's mother was sick and he was unable to coach that season, so Hal stepped in. He didn't know anything about baseball, but the man was and is a savant when it comes to people outside the home. He was so enthusiastic and even childlike. He would playfully argue with the umpires, making everyone on both teams laugh and he even told us that he would wear a dress to a game if we swept a doubleheader with our rivals, which we did and he did. Of course, there is nothing worse that a man can be than a woman.

It always baffled me that my father could be this charismatic leader outside the home and a tyrant inside it. How could someone be beloved by everyone he meets, but fly into a rage if I made a B. (The IQ Test was probably the worst thing that happened to me as a child, even worse than the physical violence. Because of that test, nothing short of perfection was allowed.) To put up an air of petit bourgeois respectability, more mimicked that practiced, but easy to foist on our working class families and churches, is profoundly confusing to a child. If I learned anything, I learned to be dishonest not only with others, but also with myself. I told myself that everything was normal and worked hard to impress institutions and individuals with our successes. We lived in the burbs, my mom didn't work outside the home, my dad was working his way up to general manager of a respected company. We were a stock that was rising, but I was miserable. I had developed a love of music, especially heavy metal and grunge because like many my age and like many families riding the wave of the 1990s tech boom, I had become disillusioned with so many things that my parents held dear and slowly began thinking for myself. Things would change for me dramatically because of important events toward the end of high school.

My high school was strange. It was a mix of new suburban kids and old farm boys and girls, but we all seemed to get along alright. The area where I was living belonged to someone with an M to begin their name but I can't remember the name. The suburb was called Big M acres and was just down the street from an honest to goodness general store where I would later work. The farm that became the suburb belonged to a man reported to be cool with a bunch of recording artists including Elvis Presley who supposedly landed his plane on the farm. Our street, Rich Drive, was named after Buddy Rich another one of the unnamed M's friends.

I was moderately popular in high school because I was perceived to be intelligent. I was always set against my friend Greg, a math wiz, in competition as to who would be the most intelligent in the school, a situation that I resent to this day.

In 1995, I was accepted to attend the National Young Leaders Conference in Washington, D.C. I had always been pretty awkward socially. I wasn't quite redneck enough for the farm boys and I wasn't quite suburban enough for the privileged kids. I was awkward looking, short, skinny, with big ears, and I didn't have much confidence. When I went to the NYLC, which was a mock Congress with people from around the US, people flocked to me. I was elected president of our group, everyone called me "Ross Perot" and was able to give a speech before the whole body.

I reckon this had a bigger effect on me than I would let on at the time. It boosted my confidence because, independently, I had succeeded. I was incredibly popular and respected, even somewhat of a mascot protected by my new found friends from places like Buffalo and San Francisco. People taught me how to act in a city and I showed my prowess at playing like a politician. It was a far cry from my suburban-rural school where I was liked, if still somewhat of a whipping boy. It was also a far cry from my father and was the first time in my life where I felt out from under his thumb.

I had been political since the fifth grade, where I used to torture my teacher about Cuba being communist. The fall of the Berlin Wall and the Soviet Union was a seminal moment in my early political life. I listened to Rush Limbaugh and Hannity, who was a host in Huntsville at the time. I was a rabid conservative. I hated feminists, environmentalists, affirmative action and pretty much anyone with flexible morals, a sensitive worldview, or who I thought didn't work hard enough. The NYLC was right up my alley and it gave me confidence that I had never before had.

My conservatism was a cry for acceptance from my father. I was never the son that he wanted. I was sensitive, critical, I talked back, and I was never perfect. My brother was definitely his favored son. He excelled at sports and education and did all the things right that I was unable to do. Conservatism and Auburn football were the primary ways that I could connect with Hal, and he relished the opportunity to tell his friends about my political prowess. Everything was about to come crashing down around my family. Our whole worldview, seemingly impenetrable, was actually built on a papier mache of lies, half-truths, unconfirmable assumptions, and ideology and my rebellion would forever change the way that my family worked. It started at church.

Shortly after my trip to D.C., I applied, with my brother, for membership in Memorial Parkway Church of Christ. I had attended for some years and was active in the youth group. My father taught there and even gave a rousing sermon until he started preaching on

Sand Mountain, the Southern terminus of the Appalachian Mountain range. I participated in the youth group's Skits With A Truth (SWAT) that performed all over the Southeast in a stripped down drama troupe that reinforced fundamentalist values. The uniforms were black, tactical jumpsuits, which was appropriate since the youth minister was a cop and firearms freak.

We were to be interviewed by the elders of the church. What happened in this interview, which I thought to be a formality, profoundly altered the course of my life. The elders grilled me for at least two hours. The question that I distinctly remember answering incorrectly was about whether or not members of the Church of Christ could collaborate with other denominations, the example that I used was in a pro-life protest. Church of Christ doctrine is that the Church of Christ is the only true church and everyone else is going to hell. The elders were concerned that, in such a protest, Church of Christ members would be influenced by other, sinful, denominations. I don't know if they ended up rejecting me or I rejecting them, but it was clear that I had no place in that church. I lost faith. I began questioning everything that I was taught.

The shock of this was so profound, so deep, so gratuitous and destructive that I doubt that I could ever adequately describe it. But, it was the best thing that ever happened to me. The church rejected me; I didn't reject the church. It gave me the freedom to acknowledge and follow my instincts that plagued my unhappy childhood. It released me from any obligation to church, family, college, morals, ideology, whatever. It was the first step toward my freedom, a freedom that I knew that I wanted, but didn't know what it was or how to get it. I am still fighting for that freedom.

I started working at Jerry's Bama Beef, a local greasy spoon, which was not my first job, but the first one that matter. My first job was working for some shithead at a local restaurant, a job arranged by my father, probably to teach me some discipline.

Jerry was different than other people in my life. He drank copiously. He smoked pot. He treated me like a human being, which was different than all other authority figures in my life up until that point. I started hanging out with the "bad" crowd who smoked, drank, and did drugs. They were all kind, down-to-Earth people. They didn't expect me to perform like a dancing monkey, just hang out, talk about nothing, and live life. It was such a shock.

The people that I was now friends with were nothing like the school, church, and family had characterized them. Why had they lied to me?

The descent into sanity was all encompassing. I rejected a scholarship to David Lipscomb University, a Church of Christ school, I mathed out all my grades my senior year so that I would know when I didn't have to work anymore, I rejected college to be an auto mechanic. The choice of auto mechanic was because I had a piece of shit 1977 CJ-5 Jeep that was always broken down and it seemed like a useful skill to know how to fix it. I still believed that if you worked hard, you would succeed and what could be harder than being a mechanic?

In my second semester of my senior year, by March, I had made high enough grades where I didn't have to do any more work. I started skipping class and going to work at Service Merchandise, a department store. My logic was that teachers and administration acted like they didn't want me at school and managers at Service Merchandise did. I went where I was wanted. In the meantime, Billy, Greg, and I were planning a cross country trip after graduation.

Three days before graduation, one of my teachers called Hal and told him that I had skipped 40 days. He was furious. It was as though I had rejected everything he stood for, I'd pissed away my future. He was right. I rejected his authority and he knew it. I'd rejected the school's authority. I'd rejected the church's authority. *They lied to me.*

My father tried his best to punish me. He tried to prevent me from walking at graduation. He tried to prevent me from going on the trip. But, I won. I understood the system underpinning education and I manipulated it to my own ends. This was the beginning of my radicalization.

The analysis of the system was something that came naturally to me. I could recognize that all of the faculty and staff had to follow certain protocols to harm students and I could easily avoid those protocols with a combination of never being around and charming my faculty members with ingratiating lies. I won't say that I am proud that I learned how to manipulate the system so easily, but I did learn a basic understanding of how bureaucratic systems worked and a trenchant disgust for them. No one reached out to me, including my parents, to see what was wrong. They just thought it was a stage. Honestly, I didn't even know what was wrong; I just knew that I was profoundly unhappy with the way things were and I set out to work the system for my own benefit. Theoretically, I could have used this information much like I did as a teenager - to enrich myself, but, as I would later learn, the system wasn't so much about me, but about how all people are subject to these systems and that they are profoundly dehumanizing. My complete disregard for the system didn't indicate some underlying problem to my institutional overlords, but of my immorality and sinfulness in abandoning these systems that everyone depends on. I found them unnecessary.

Of course, the impetus for such a disregard was the implicit anarchism in Southern culture. We hate these protocols by nature, prima facie. No one is ever going to tell us what to do and if they try we will fuck them up or kill them. The only thing holding us together is high-minded notions of loyalty, which have been the source of much violence, unnecessarily, for perceived slights to one's honor and loyalty. The working class culture that I was about to enter into would be such a snug fit that it is probably the most comfortable, relaxed, and proud that I had ever been. Rednecks think we're ungoverned, yet we blame our problems on black people and women because, since we are ungoverned, it couldn't possible be the government and their allies because they have no power over us. All our problems are cultural and identitarian, never political or economic, because in those realms, we get what we fucking deserve. It's anarchism wrapped in toxic masculinity, white supremacy, and, of course, The Stars and Stripes and The Stars and Bars.

The summer of 1996 was one of absolute debauchery. We were committing low level vandalism on mailboxes throughout our community. The neighbor to the girl I was dating had a John Deere mailbox that I stole and burned. During the trip to California, one of my friends brought an ounce of marijuana and we left a trail of vandalism from here to San Francisco. All of this criming while white was profoundly stupid. We could have ended up in prison or worse. The ATF even came to one of my friends' house after he stole a mailbox and blew it up with a pipe bomb he made out of an empty CO_2 canister and gunpowder from a bullet.

The trip, as it became known, was quite an adventure. We decided to go to Mexico while we were in El Paso. We stashed the weed in a cemetery and headed across the border. Roads are a little different in Mexico and we ended up quite lost. To our chagrin all of the road signs are written in Spanish making our return to the States somewhat problematic. Eventually we found ourselves, at 3 am, on what resembled an interstate. I looked back after we passed a sign and it said "El Paso, TX, USA" the opposite direction we were going. We are damn lucky we didn't end up in Monterrey. We got back to the USA, scooped the weed and headed west. Tombstone was fairly uneventful except for being dead tired and language snafus. Headed out of Tombstone, we were searched by border patrol who put his hand on the bag with the weed in it, but eventually let us go. Criming while white. We also broke down in Lubbock, received aid from a local woman, and found out that the insurance plan had roadside assistance after pushing the 1994 Cutlass at least a mile in the hot ass Texas sun.

Does this have a point? We were all profoundly angry. What was this that we had been put through? 13 years of teachers barking out orders, of parents telling us how life is, of lies, bald faced, ridiculous lies. We wanted to take it out on something. We wanted revenge.

Revenge is one thing. Focused, righteous anger is another. Greg and I went to Lollapalooza in East Tennessee that summer. One of the bands performing was Rage Against the Machine. I had listened to them in the past and some of their lyrics stuck with me - bulls on parade, fuck you, I won't do what you tell me. Now I'm driving down Rodeo with a shotgun/these people ain't seen a brown skinned man since they granddaddy bought one.

Nixon had just died. Zach de la Rocha sent him off well. "Fuck Richard Nixon, I'm glad that mother fucker is dead and in the ground." What struck me was not necessarily what he said, but the freedom and confidence with which he said it. I wanted some of that. I really didn't even know what I was listening to, but my political education had begun.

When we returned home, I threw a party at my parents' house that was lame, but my brother covered for me with the folks. After the party, Greg and Billy stuck around. We were outside and I picked up my gold TPX baseball bat and walked straight to my parents mailbox and smashed the shit out of it. There was nothing that I had done up to that point in my life that had been this fulfilling.

CLASS

My parents kicked me out at 18. If I wasn't going to college, I had to survive on my own. I had been working at a general store and going to school at a local community college studying auto mechanics. The program was supposed to be an hour of instruction and 7 hours of hands on experience. In practice, it was an hour of instruction and 7 hours of standing the fuck around. I befriended a gear head that had two hot rods. I started skipping out on class and riding around in his Chevelle, smoking Camels, and pretending to work on cars.

I got a peace sign tattooed on my right shoulder, which I didn't tell my parents about because they would have flipped. When I was wearing a tank top one day, my mom noticed it and would later tell me that I finally had some peace, an insight that was spot on. My life had been tumultuous as a child with lots of moving from place to place, difficulty fitting in, expectations that should have never been placed on a child, loss of faith and values, and a deep sense that something was not right. Everything became simple - friends and work, and that was the lot of it. I went to work and got a paycheck every week, and though, I'd eventually become tired of the tyranny of the boss, the simplicity of my new life allowed me some space to sort things out.

My political education came to a grinding halt. I was focused on earning a living and living a fairly simple life without too many encumbrances. I had a girlfriend that I was terrible to. My family had been rigidly patriarchal and it would be years before I would even hear the term feminism. It's not something that I'm proud of, but it is the truth.

My ineptness with women was rooted in my upbringing in a rigidly fundamentalist church where women were not allowed to speak or teach and basically were to cook, clean, and care for children. After I was baptised as a child, women teachers could no longer lead the classes I was in. I, as a saved male, was higher in the hierarchy than seasoned women three times my age. My logic in dating women was always to establish my masculinity and power and to have the women follow my lead. None of this was conscious, but just the way things were supposed to be and I wouldn't even start to be critical of it until I was in college.

I spent much time after moving out with Philip, a friend from high school. I moved to one of the "worst" neighborhoods in Huntsville that white folks called "Little Harlem." Philip smoked weed while I did not and mostly we just played Magic: the Gathering. I didn't start smoking weed until Daniel, a dedicated couch surfer with a big rig driving father, convinced me to one Saturday afternoon. I got really dizzy and vomited chili-cheese fries in my sink. Daniel was dating some well-to-do high school sophomore, who clearly was doing it to piss her parents off.

As far as cities in the South go, Huntsville was fairly progressive owing to a robust tech industry fueled by Redstone Arsenal which built rocket and missile systems. The huge federal subsidy afforded by Redstone Arsenal meant that Huntsville was a fairly affluent city without the deep segregation and poverty of Birmingham. The racial tensions, while clearly still very much a part of the social fabric, weren't nearly as thick as in a place like Birmingham. But this may be because of a more effective white cultural hegemony than Birmingham instead of any real relief. The area also had a high number of PhDs per capita and many international residents because of the Arsenal and the tech sector, which led to a much more cosmopolitan and less provincial sensibility than other areas in the South.

Daniel was in and out of my life, but Phil was pretty consistent. Our daily routine was to meet at my apartment after work and play either Super Street Fighter 2 or Magic the Gathering or both. Magic became a pretty serious hobby for me and I started playing in local tournaments. At one of these tournaments I met Jason who would become a friend of almost 20 years. He invited us to his farm, which was about 30 miles outside of Huntsville on top of Merrill Mountain. It was a beautiful place and became a source of respite for many years.

Phil once remarked that Magic the Gathering taught him his vocabulary. I'm not sure if it taught me my vocabulary, but it did teach me practical math, strategy, and tactics. The game is about constructing a deck of a magical monsters and spells and pitting your deck against others. It was a fun game and a good place for a awkward young adult to meet other awkward, brilliant young adults. My mom took us to a tournament in Florida and remarked at the intellectual firepower represented by these gamers and led me to wonder why so many brilliant young men (and it was almost exclusively men) would spend all of their time playing a collectible card game. The game itself was sort of a rip-off. They came out with new cards every year and you had to have four of each to legitimately have a chance to compete. There is no telling how much money I spent on that damn game as a young man.

One of the themes of my early adulthood was the search for male role models, since clearly, I did not see eye to eye with my father. Gary became one such role model as my boss at the auto shop. He was patient and rolled with the punches. Nothing was ever a crisis and the stability helped me greatly. Being an auto mechanic requires a great deal of patience. It's hot, dirty, and, rarely do things go right. I never had much patience, much like my father, and have struggled with patience all my life. But, Gary was an example of patience, especially with me, a person who knew very little about cars, didn't have a great work ethic, and had a quick temper.

Another such role model was Jason's dad, who was a fiery redneck liberal who hated Rush Limbaugh. He always tried to engage me in political discussion, but I didn't care. He was also divorcing Jason's mom, Janie, living off the farm, and digging a pond with a box blade, which was basically stress relief. Jason's dad, Jerry was one of the most important influences in my life. He owned a machine shop and interacted with his children like they were adults. He allowed them to make their own decisions, encouraged critical thinking, and, ultimately, was a great teacher.

The story that I remember vividly when first meeting Jerry was that I told him that I was a conservative. He asked me how I felt about hand guns. I said, "we should throw them all to the bottom of the ocean." He said, "you're liberal." The interaction was one that I would always remember because it was the first time that a white, working class man had ever said that it was ok to not be conservative. Over the years, I've probably grown much more radical and don't have the same loyalty to the Democratic Party that Jerry had because New Deal policies brought his father, the original owner of Bowman's, Jerry's business, out of poverty. The connection with the Democrats was linked to his connection with his father who built something out of nothing. I respect Jerry tremendously even to this day.

Added to this positive influence was an extremely tight knit group of friends made of high school cohorts, their girlfriends, and their girlfriends' friends. My life was rich with relationships and fellowship. All of my free time was spent with friends, most of them working class and only vaguely religious. If I wasn't at the drag strip, I was smoking weed and playing Magic, wake-boarding on Lake Guntersville, or just chilling with whomever.

For the first time in my life, things were simple. Work, friends, work, friends. I was making decent money for a young, single man and developing a powerful taste for buffalo wings. I can't overstate how different this environment was from my family life. I had no "potential," no expectation and no pressure to be the best. For the first time in my life, I was comfortable.

Mo & Alicia

Mo was a California raised Latino who worked at a local four wheel drive shop close to the shop in which I worked. He was also a small time drug dealer who knew all the local police. His girlfriend, Alicia, was an educated black woman, and pretty out-of-place in the circles we ran in. I had grown my hair out long and Alicia often braided it. These were my first friends of color since grade school. One of Mo's coworker's was named Bobby and he was an ex-con who lived in a trailer south of Madison. They always played this game where customers would come in saying racist shit about black people and eventually Mo would show a picture of his girlfriend to the customer. Bobby played like he wasn't racist, but when he took me aside at his house to show me pornography of black women and white men, I was pretty creeped out.

There were always shenanigans at the off road shop. After purchasing paintball guns, Mo was going to show us how he could shoot through the open windows of a moving car. So, one of the customers rolled down both back windows and drove down the street. Mo accomplished his task - shot through both windows of a moving car. Too bad he hit another car coming the other direction. The owner of that car pressed charges and Mo went to jail for discharging a firearm in the city limits. Drug dealer goes down for shooting a paintball gun. Ain't that some shit?

Years later, after Mo and Alicia broke up, I ran into Alicia and asked her out to my friends New Years Eve Party. The party was alright and my white friends didn't say too much stuff that was offensive. Alicia drank too much champagne and threw up in the snow in the back yard. I took her home in the snow and we went on a few more dates. I was unprepared to date interracially. When she said that black men at the restaurant were looking at her because of me, I didn't understand. When she wouldn't hold my hand in public, I didn't understand. I just didn't understand. She was a very nice, intelligent woman that I was unprepared to date.

Dating interracially is a source of discussion among both whites and blacks in the South. Unlike other parts of the country, there are still strong taboos against interracial dating. My grandmother once told me that she was against it because she would say "what about the kids?" I guess suggesting that they would be confused. This attitude is common among elders, but even younger folks have strong feelings against it. I'm not against interracial marriage by any stretch of the imagination, but, from my very limited experience, there must be understanding and openness about all of the problematic stuff that goes along with it, especially in the South. I guess this is true with any marriage, but my single foray into interracial dating was coupled with a profound ignorance of what it means to be a person of color and, in my desire to make everything simple, I glossed over what could have been, at the very least, an important learning experience. Instead, I just broke up with her and moved on.

The last time I saw Mo, he was a bouncer at a strip club.

The Clique

The clique is kinda hard to describe. In many ways, it was profoundly toxic and closed off. It consisted of Greg and his partner Shirley, Sam, Phil and his partner Amy, Billy, Rob, and myself. For most of the folks in the clique, these were their only real friends. Many of them worked together, spending most of their waking time with the same people. I had known the core folks since I was an adolescent and ended up living with Billy, which was a disaster. The key feature of the clique was hostility toward outsiders, so much so that none of my other friends wanted to associate with them. There were rivalries and slights and factions, all of it underpinned by a weird sexuality that centered around Shirley. She and Greg were the alphas since they had the most money and the house to host the gatherings.

Before the partners, the group was all male and stalked clubs looking for women, which none of us were ever lucky enough to bag. So, we went home, talked shit, and got hammered. After Fight Club came out, we even fought each other. Clearly the sexuality preceded Shirley.

As I got older, I became more and more disengaged with this group. They seemed stuck in high school, which was fine for them, but high school had been a terrible experience for me. I wanted to meet new people and new types of people. The straw that broke the camel's back was when Greg got arrested for possession of LSD. There was another arrest a few months later, but nothing seemed to come of it. Shirley's father was a sheriff and when I was at a local restaurant a couple of years later, I bumped into Kevin, a childhood friend who was on work release. He said that Greg, his friend from childhood, set him up, which was what the second arrest was about. Kevin had a wife and child. Greg went on to become wealthy as an engineer. These were not the people that I wanted to be around. I'd choose the honest drug dealer any day.

Jason & Brian

I met Jason, Jerry's son, when I was 19 and he was still in high school. He went to a tiny rural school in Northeast Alabama. He became one of my closest friends and still is to this day. We met during his parents' divorce; after the divorce, Jason moved to a suburb of Huntsville and attended a pretty rough urban school. It was there that he met Brian, a savvy and worldly football player who kept Jason from getting killed.

Jason didn't handle the transition well. Good natured and kind at heart, he agreed to everything that people asked him to do. He had wild parties at his mother's house that always ended with the cops being called and at least once with someone unloading a .45 into the garage. By the time, he had graduated, much of this had calmed down, and I avoided most of it as I was more interested in maintaining a low profile.

After Jason graduated, he befriended his sister's boyfriend, Mike, who was probably one of the smartest people I have ever met. They both became engrossed in the local poker world, playing in games at bars across the city and eventually hosting their own game. I played when I could. When I did play at Jason's house there was a steady stream of customers from Mike's drug business throughout the night. Both Jason and Mike became pretty well known and accomplished poker players in the area, but Mike is significantly better because of his patience and discipline.

Brian took a different path. He worked in restaurants from the time he graduated high school until now. He is a manager of a local restaurant. Brian's biggest vice was women, and he appeared to have a new girlfriend every time I saw him. As someone who was so patriarchal that even women raised in the patriarchy thought I was shit, I always admired Brian's ability to connect with women, even if some of it was bullshit. Brian was always at Jason's wild parties and on numerous occasions probably prevented someone from getting killed or badly hurt.

The time in my life was one of comfortable confusion. Fundamentalist religion always shaped my thinking. In fundamentalism, everything is clear, everything makes sense, but for me, the only thing that made sense were my friends. I dabbled in churches during my early adulthood, even experimenting with Pentecostal faith, which is heavily rooted in the working class. Nothing stuck. Clearly, I was looking for something, but what I kept returning to was fellowship and genuine love and friendship with other people. There was a stark simplicity to the meaning of love and friendship that has colored my future political engagement.

I don't underestimate the effect and value of Jason and Bryan in my life. They taught me the meaning of friendship and solidarity. They were always there through everything, they called me on my shit, and they suggested that I get help when I needed it. In a world where true friendship is ephemeral and relationships are temporary and transactional, I'm truly blessed to have people in my life that are not family, but might as well be. Bryan even served as treasurer in the first organization I created. In a life of transition and change such as mine, constants are rare, but of the utmost importance because they are a constantly reminder of where I came from and to remember my roots no matter who I turn into next.

Jules & Sam

I knew Jules from Memorial Parkway Church of Christ where he attended as much for pleasing his parents as for scaring the piss out of the church leadership. He had earrings, a nose ring, unconventional if self-aggrandizing views, and he was striking with olive skin and a strong jaw. The ladies loved him. He started hanging out with the clique, but never really fit in because he was a number of years older. One of the funniest things that I have ever seen was when we were doing Fight Club, Jules told Billy, "I want you to hit me as hard as you can" like the movie. We told him to shut the fuck up, but he insisted. Billy knocked his ass out cold.

When he woke up, he was giggling uncontrollably. Dude probably still has brain damage. Hilarious.

Jules moved in with Sam in a house in Five Points. I think that they were both working retail and Sam was dating an older woman with a kid, but I don't remember their names. Sam had a 1977 Ford Bronco with a lift kit and big tires. We spent a lot of time on off-road trails when we were hanging out, even traveling a couple times to Tellico ORV on the Tennessee-North Carolina border. We loved doing outdoorsy stuff such as camping, which they introduced me to, rock climbing and off-roading. Sam and I even went down to Auburn to stay with a woman that he was dating and watch an Auburn football game. I also spent many Friday nights with them at a local coffee shop that sold beer and at numerous clubs. Both of them did a lot of club drugs, coke, ecstasy, and others, but while I smoked a lot of weed, I wouldn't touch the harder stuff. There were always women at the house, which was one of the reasons that I liked to go, but it was clear that they weren't interested in me, a sort of sheltered, wannabe hippy with lingering Christian values.

Jules and I are still friends and give each other shit constantly on Facebook. I've known him probably 25 years. Sam I've lost touch with over the years. The last thing that I heard about him, he was a mountain bike pro or some shit like that. At this time in my life, having friends was the most important thing to me. They served as a sort of surrogate family while I learned to live in a world that was much broader than my parents ever told me. I was learning to live with moral ambiguity, with good people making bad decisions or questionable decisions or just decisions that weren't like what I thought the decisions of adulthood were or should be. Living and socializing with working class people of all stripes taught me that the world was complex and that I didn't know where I fit and that that was perfectly alright.

Betsy

Betsy was the consistent woman in my life. Friends with Billy, Betsy knew all of my friends and wove in and out of my life in six month stints. She even dated some of my mechanic friends. Her easy, laid back attitude, her no bullshit personality, and her love of cars drew me to her. I probably had a crush on her, but was inept with women and didn't want to lose a friend, so nothing ever happened. She did revel in my ineptness with relationships. When I brought one woman that I was dating to the drag strip, only to sit three rows below another woman that I was dating, she made fun of me for years. Her boyfriend was a terror and threatened me with physical violence on a number of occasions.

The first night in my first apartment, at a party there, she told me that she had been raped, kidnapped, and subsequently had an abortion. I would not come close to understanding the trust in me required for her to tell me that until years later. Besides the conversation was broken up by law enforcement who told us that folks need to leave or we need to quiet down. Betsy was the only woman that I was truly comfortable with in my early adulthood.

At 18, and coming out of a fundamentalist Christian culture where abortion was the ultimate sin, the reveal from Betsy, which she did because someone told me that she had an abortion and she wanted me to know the situation, shook me more than I care to admit. Now, with current eyes, I see a bit more clearly. There was no way that I could blame her for having an abortion considering the situation that she was in. From the lips of a real person, my friend, telling me about having an abortion and why she had it, I couldn't possibly condemn her. While I wasn't exactly a feminist, my reeducation about the way the world worked opened my eyes to the difficult dilemmas that people, many of whom were my friends, faced and would face in their life. Betsy was profoundly concerned that I would condemn her for having an abortion, but I just became more confused, which, at this point in my life, was a good thing.

My work life, which was virtually divorced from my personal life, was an education in exploitation and oppression and a signal of my growing madness.

I began working at a shop in central Huntsville when I was 19. I had no idea what I was doing; I didn't even know how to push the piston back on a brake caliper. I got the job because the owner of the shop came into the general store in which I was working and I asked him for a job. No interview, no background check, no qualifications. If anyone tells you that there are no benefits to being white, they are flat out lying or they are stupid.

Probably half of the cars and trucks that I worked on my first six months came back on a chain. But, after six months I began to pick up the tricks and the muscle memory needed to actually be a mechanic. I was learning about strong and gentle masculinity from Gary, who clearly loved his wife deeply and didn't try to control her and the same with Don, the company's owner, though he suggested that his wife was high maintenance. All of this was shot through with gender politics that I was completely unaware existed.

I quickly became a fairly talented mechanic; it turns out that my community college professor was right and that I was a quick learner. I did have potential. But, I had run up a sizable debt with the Snap On man who comes by every shop and sells tools. I bought tons and I bought the best ones. I was struggling to feed myself. I had to find a higher paying job and sadly leave a place that had stabilized my life and provided me with male role models when I needed them the most.

I found myself in the employ of a tire shop next to Madison Square Mall. It was my first time to be on piece wage instead of salary and I made good money my first month - ten dollars an hour in 1998. Things changed dramatically after the first month. I was changing tires and oil, doing basic maintenance with few repairs. This wouldn't have been so bad, but Firestone cooked the books. Instead of paying based on Chilton's guide, the industry standard, Firestone had their own books that paid much less per job, sometimes by hundreds of dollars. In essence, the discount that customers got by using Firestone was paid by the worker, the individual mechanic.

On top of the cooked books, management was highly disciplinary and oppressive. Mechanics were routinely asked to work two or three hours later than scheduled, but if they showed up late to work were written up. 70 hour work weeks were common and the physical nature of the job and the hours took a toll on my body. I was also making less money, close to minimum wage. One Saturday, I was particularly bedraggled partially because of the work and partially because I was staying up later and later and smoking more and more weed. Paul, the general manager, told me what I guess was some form of pep talk by saying that he didn't care if his beloved Middle Tennessee State University won or lost as long as they played hard, suggesting that I needed to play harder. I told him, "football players play hard for three hours a week." That was probably the beginning of the end for me there.

I did have some friends at Firestone: Booker, a laid back black guy who drank beer all day, Nacho (real name Ignacio but folks just called him Nacho) and his son-in-law, Felipe. I bought weed from Booker and Nacho and Felipe kept me fed on the tight weeks.

And then there was Kelly, a white good-ole-boy, who was probably one of the best mechanics that I'd ever met. But, he had an alcohol and drug problem as serious as I'd ever seen and he was routinely drunk and coked up at work.

Booker left a few months into my tenure, but I ended up selling him my car for $400 and $600 worth of weed, which was top quality. He hung out with me and Phil on numerous occasions. Nacho err up speaking to Paul about his attitude and soon found himself doing landscaping for another company, and Felipe ended up in trouble with the law. What kind of trouble, I don't know, but I got the distinct idea that it had to do with discrimination. Kelly finally ended up using all his get out of jail free cards when he came to work one Saturday so fucked up that he couldn't even install a thermostat. The last time I saw him he had cleaned up quite a bit, lost some weight, and was looking for a job. He seemed happy. I was glad for him because he was a truly good dude as were Booker, Nacho, and Felipe. They made life at Firestone bearable.

After about a year, I had had enough. I had a lead on a job in Southeast Huntsville. During lunch, I packed up my tools and left. Fuck you Firestone.

During this time, I was on and off dating a woman named Desireah, who looked exactly like Pink, the pop singer. In some ways, she was my dream woman as far as appearance - edgy, dark, and mysterious. I treated her poorly, which is why we were on again off again. I basically believed that women should do what men say and as a result only had a few, short relationships. I was still technically a virgin, though I had fooled around with a number of women. Part of this was because of my awkwardness and misogyny, and part of this was because of lingering Christian ideas.

I bounced around from terrible job to terrible job for a couple of years, even going backward from being a mechanic to a mere tire jockey. I moved home for a little while and then moved in with Billy.

I got out of auto mechanics completely. I went to work for my father at Halsey Grocery Company, third shift. I started by loading trucks and my supervisor was this gigantic black man, Dexter. Dexter purported to be a Christian, but told the raunchiest and most off color stories imaginable. I suppose it endeared him to the young men that he led, which were about half black and half white. This was my first real experience with racial politics. I had worked with black folks before, but had never been led by them. The first day, Sterling stopped me while I was loading a truck and asked me point blank if I was racist, to which I said no. I was also asked if I liked hip-hop music and certain types of food. The black guys, Don Juan, Sterling, and others were trying to see what kind of white person I was, and I'm sure the answer that they came up with was "oblivious." But, I made friends and even smoked weed with white and black workers together. My father found out about it and threatened to drug test everyone, which basically meant that I couldn't hang out with anyone from work anymore. It's hard to overstate how naive I was, particularly with the advantages that I had as the white, general manager's son, which is probably the only reason that I survived the job as long as I did.

My parents were doing well as part of probably the last generation in which hard work actually paid off. It did not pay off for me, though my instability was a harbinger of things to come. Everyone I knew thought I was a little crazy.

On September 11, 2001, four months before my father and I would leave Halsey (I didn't want to leave, but when he did, it was made clear that I was no longer welcome), a group of Middle Eastern people flew two planes into the Twin Towers, knocking them down. It happened just as I was returning home from work. I was shaken since I lived walking distance from Redstone Arsenal and within sight of US Missile Defense Command. The reaction of all my friends was striking. My middle class friends took off work and watched TV all day and my working class friends went to work unphased.

My reaction turned to curiosity. I had continued to listen to Rage Against the Machine over the years and it was clear that the Middle Eastern fighters were not just crazed desert people. They had a reason, even if it was a bad one. This led from one rabbit hole to another with me thinking something along the lines of "I've got to do more with my life than I'm doing." I decided to go to Auburn University, my father's alma mater. A big reason that I wanted to go there was because I was and am a rabid Auburn Football fan. I was going to major in biology or something, but that changed shortly after I got there.

Over these years, my political education was more or less dormant, aside from learning the value of genuine community and of how terrible working class life really is, which I guess isn't really dormant, but it would not be overt again until I was in college. To be working class in the South is to keep your head down and follow orders - to be a robot. It was the culture that I rejected as a teen and was being reimposed as an adult. My madness was growing, marked by instability and the inability to function as a worker. College seemed like a line of flight to freedom. I would spend many years there chasing that freedom.

I also learned that there is a stark diversity in realities. My family always prided itself in being the All American Family. We put on the facade of patriotism, suburbia, respectability, and wholesomeness and we pretended like that was the only legitimate way to live. I quickly learned that it was not and that for some folks, reality was illicit drugs, shitty jobs, and fleeting relationships; but most importantly I realized that those realities were just as valid as anything that I had been taught was superior.

Consciousness is material in nature. My material reality and my relationships with other people created my consciousness. I sought simplicity and love. I longed for a better life and believed that hard work would lead to it for most of my life. The redneck value of hard work betrays the redneck existence. It keeps us working in a way that supposedly predicts financial success, but never actually leads there. The next paycheck, the big break was just around the corner. But, hard work leads to freedom; it is a kind of anarchy of hard work. That weekly paycheck gives the illusion of self-sufficiency and self-determination at least until it runs out and then it's on to working for the next one. The second biggest lie of redneck culture aside from white supremacy is that work equals freedom. Work should equal freedom, but this is co-opted under capitalism.

With the September 11 attacks, I knew something was wrong. I didn't know what it was and I went to college to figure it out. My political education was reignited.

Late in 2001, I met Sarah, the worst mistake of my life.

STUDENT

I met Sarah at a gas station after work. She sat behind me during homeroom in high school and I always thought she was attractive in a punk rock kind of way. She invited me to go to church with her and I accepted. It was the beginning of three and a half years of misery. I was working as a tire jockey, but only temporarily because I was going to Auburn in the fall.

Sarah's theory of men was that if you keep them well laid, they will do anything you want and I was perfectly amenable to this theory since I'd never had steady sex in my entire life. The beginning was incredibly hot and most of my vices - smoking, drinking, and weed - didn't seem to bother her. She had a strange puritanical streak that seemed to keep her off the opiates from which she was about six months clean, but it didn't seem to be targeted at me.

We got engaged about six weeks later, told all the relatives, booked the church, and started ordering invitations.

One night she told me that I needed to quit smoking and that "if I loved her, I would quit." I said no and she turned around to leave, presumably for good. In that moment, a million things went through my mind - the embarrassment of telling my parents that Sarah left, how sorry I felt for her because she had a rough life, the ceding of my autonomy to another person, and the lack of partner to go to Auburn with. I stopped her and said that I would quit smoking. If I had it to do over again, I would have let her walk out the door and never return. Threatening to leave became the most potent weapon in Sarah's emotional warfare.

We got married at an Episcopal Church in June in a beautiful wedding. I pulled my dreadlocks up for the wedding. Yes, I had dreadlocks; I'm not proud of it, but I did. We were the perfect hippy-punk couple and everyone thought we were destined for a positive future. Sarah yelled at me for thirty minutes on our honeymoon because she didn't have an orgasm during sex. To say that our relationship was rocky or volatile would be an understatement. We fought often. She punched me in the ear and spit in my face in the first six months. She told me regularly that if I didn't behave, she would leave me. So I behaved. I felt sorry for her. She was an addict with little experience of any sort of stability going back to her childhood. So, I let her abuse me.

She asked me once a week when we were going to have a child.

In retrospect, the way I felt in my marriage to Sarah was similar to how I felt living under my father's roof. It wasn't desperation so much as resignation that this was my life and this was what I had to deal with. I escaped through education and college football. As I have said before, like many Southerners, college football was a huge part of my life. Students got heavily discounted tickets and I almost never missed a home game, usually going by myself owing to my isolation of being in an abusive marriage and being 25% older than all of my classmates. Football was a great respite; I knew everything about the players, tutored one, and religiously listened to sports talk radio. My six years at Auburn were some of the most successful in Auburn football history (we beat Alabama all six years that I was there) due mostly to the strong coaching of Tommy Tuberville, who cut his teeth at Ole Miss and was known affectionately as "The Riverboat Gambler."

I transferred from Huntsville to a mechanic job in Opelika, which is just east of Auburn. I worked for two days and quit. I wasn't doing that shit anymore. I was going to be an educated man.

Right before school started, I traveled to Birmingham to see Desmond Tutu speak. By this time, Dubya was beating the drums of war and Tutu undressed him publicly, which struck me in a very similar way to Zach de la Rocha many years before. I asked if the food at the table was indigenous to South Africa and an Auburn student at the table scoffed at the notion. It was from South Africa. I would get this in college on more than a few occasions. Folks' assumptions about the way that I talk and dress were quickly destroyed. I took great pride in doing this. After the speech by the Archbishop, I thought I might want to be a priest. I began attending a local Episcopal Church.

I loved college. It was a welcome relief from a terrible marriage and introduced me to ideas that seemed to make sense. During my first semester, I took an Introduction to Anthropology class. The concept of cultural relativism struck me as quite useful. Of all the people I'd known with numerous, sometimes criminal habits, it was a great relief to judge them by their own standards. By the standards of the church that I grew up in, everyone I knew was going to hell. Cultural relativism removed that burden.

Cultural relativism is something that I use often in my activism today. There are many different and diverse types of activists and many spend their days attacking each other for being ideologically not up to snuff. A little dose of cultural relativism would at least lend some understanding not only to the reasoning behind seemingly regressive ideas, but also to people perceived as opponents who may have different ideas. It lends itself to more systematic critiques of powerful institutions because the culture of the oppressed, which is rarely progressive, arises in a cauldron of oppression. Some oppressive beliefs have strong reasons behind them rooted in the destruction of people's communities.

I made straight As my first two years while I was not working for money. I also attempted to start the process of becoming a priest, but Sarah intentionally sabotaged the interview with the rector. I started the process of becoming a priest because I wanted, vaguely, to be like Desmond Tutu. I was just dipping my toe into fights for justice, and, mostly subconsciously, I thought that the priesthood was an avenue for this, much like I would think that professorship was a similar avenue later in life. Sarah attended the meeting with the rector under protest and acted sullen and displeased throughout the whole process. I was humiliated and gave up on religion completely. Sarah wanted me to be a biology teacher so that was what I was going to be. What I wanted didn't matter. I wanted to be an Anthropologist.

I started working at Domino's delivering pizzas in my four wheel drive 1982 Toyota Hilux and through an online forum met Patrick who had a 1970s International Scout. I still had dreadlocks and he invited me to help him get his Scout running. Dude didn't really know what to think of me when I showed up in overalls with a six pack of Miller High Life, but we got his Scout running; the timing was bad out of whack, and we spent the rest of the day talking shit and sharing stories. Patrick was pretty young and came from an affluent section of suburban Atlanta and the two of us were about as different as folks could get.

Patrick became a close friend and I even asked him to be a groomsman at my second wedding, but he could not attend because he could not afford a ticket from Portland to Birmingham. We smoked a lot of weed together and often listened to music in his house in a college kids' neighborhood in Auburn. We also worked on four wheel drive trucks, drinking beer, and male-bonding. I was quite a bit older than Patrick who struggled in college not because he was unintelligent, but because he never went to class and didn't see the value in education. He reminded me of myself at that age, questioning conventional wisdom, his place in the world, and relying on friendship to get him through day-by-day. I think my working class, practical sensibilities appealed to him and drew a sharp contrast from his evangelical upbringing. Patrick ended up leaving school, working for a fabricator, and eventually coming back and excelling in his degree. Having grown up quite a bit, he told me how stupid he felt because college wasn't that hard with a little application.

I began exploring more deeply about who I was and was beginning to learn that in limited ways, I could mold and shape who I was. A core literature class in Women's Studies was a large contributor to my newfound consciousness. We read Pride and Prejudice, which I thought was boring, and something by Sandra Cisneros that was amazing. But, what I distinctly remember was reading Vanity Fair which suggested that no one can ever fully escape what society says they are. As a redneck auto mechanic from Alabama, that notion stuck with me until this day in understanding how others perceive me. It would serve me well in reading contexts of everything from a bonfire to a board room.

The feminist education probably further undermined my marriage. If women didn't have to have gender roles, then neither did men. If men didn't have to have gender roles, then i didn't have to do what my wife told me to do and I didn't have to be a high school teacher. To be fair, college changed me dramatically and I was becoming a person that my wife didn't want to be married to, which was not my wife's fault. We tried counseling, which helped, but it didn't change the fact that we were two very different people that wanted very different things out of life.

Late in our marriage we were down a car. I needed the car to go to the library and my wife needed the car to go to her workout. She screamed at me for at least an hour and repeatedly hit me on the head with a plastic Coke bottle. What happened next was the worst thing that I had ever done in my life. I was emotionally broken by this point in our marriage and I finally snapped, though there is no justification for what I did. I pushed her down and screamed at her repeatedly "do you want me to be a bad husband?"

In that moment, I became my father. I became everything that I never wanted to be. The reason I didn't go to college and quit church was because I didn't want to be my parents who were brutal, but in that moment all that running away didn't matter. A few months later, Sarah came home and asked me to bring in the groceries. I did not. She said that she wanted a divorce, which she said often. I told her at earlier times when she said that she wanted a divorce that one day, she's going to say that and I'm going to pack my shit up and leave and never come back. On this day, that happened. It was January. We signed divorce papers and never talked again. Last time I heard she was living back in Huntsville close to her mom. It was the worst three and a half years of my life.

After leaving our house, I stopped at a convenience store and bought two packs of Marlboro Menthol Lights. Buying these cigarettes was an act of profound resistance and freedom to me. I could never again be told who I was going to be or what I could do with my life. In that instance, I reconnected fully with the implicit anarchism of redneck culture. While tortured relationships with women are common in redneck mythology (just listen to bluegrass), my relationship with Sarah had gone beyond the battle-of-the-sexes and into emotional manipulation and abuse. It was a toxic situation that I was ultimately glad to be rid of.

During the divorce, I took a class in rural sociology. The professor, Conner, sent out an invitation to apply for a mentee/mentor fellowship to do research in rural sociology. I jumped at the opportunity. I needed something to get my mind off my terrible personal life and deep sadness about my failed marriage. I had also decided that I was going to be an anthropologist, so this gave me the opportunity to try my hand at research. When I met with Conner about the fellowship for the first time, he said something to the effect of "are you ready to fight the man?" I said absolutely. Little did I know that my life would be forever changed.

At the end of the class, we read a book called Streets of Hope about the Dudley Street Neighborhood Initiative that changed my life. It was about a group of regular folk in Boston who took control of their neighborhood and built a life for themselves. It resonated with my new found left-wing radicalism and with my redneck sensibilities of "do for self." These folks were even granted the power of eminent domain by the city to seize illegal dumping properties from unscrupulous developers. They turned those waste lands into permanently affordable housing. I knew then that I wanted to have something to do with community development for the rest of my life. Hell, I even got to meet the executive director of DSNI in June of 2016 when he came as a consultant to Birmingham. He was not impressed with us at all.

It is hard to put into words what Conner did for me. Had it not been for him, I would have never finished college and the path of my life would have been starkly different. I had already become radical through studying anthropology, particularly reading Foucault and Marx. But, it was unfocused and undisciplined and I didn't understand it that well. Conner didn't so much tell me how to understand social theory as he did give me the opportunity to be myself. Nothing like that ever happened in my life until Conner. It was transformative. I did a shitty job with the research because I basically read theory and hung out with old friends from Huntsville, in which the reconnection with the past served as a healing salve.

During this research, one of my friends from Huntsville, Rob, committed suicide. He had bipolar disorder and went off his meds at the request of a woman he was in love with, or at least this is the rumor. He was a member of my dysfunctional group from high school. I did not want to go to the funeral. It was unbelievably

strange. The group was in a state of shock. People asked me if I

was moving back in a daze of loss and confusion. I realized how

much I had changed. When I left five years earlier, I was a

struggling auto mechanic looking for a break. Now, I was becoming

a star student, which was not a mantra that I relished, but it did

change my perspective. The dysfunction of the group became

readily apparent; the competition, the sexual power plays, the back-

biting, and gossip finally destroyed the group - all went their

separate ways, and in many respects, Rob saved them from

themselves. It was a community gone way wrong. A close friend

told me that if I didn't get control of my mental health that I was

going to end up like Rob.

I met Conner at one of the most profoundly transformative

moments in my life, a moment when my social position shifted from

firmly working class to bourgeois intellectual. The transformation

was difficult and on a couple of occasions I embarrassed myself in

public because I didn't know the rules of academia. I was in a

feminist talk and discussion and I said that I wanted male birth

control, to which the speaker responded that I should check out

Men's Studies. I didn't even know it was an insult until years later. I was always flirting with other academic women, which was fairly mundane behavior for the working class, but just slightly frowned upon by the rigid rules of academic behavior.

It would be easy to understate the level of patience that my mentors had to have with me during this time. To say that I was eccentric was an understatement and to say that I had imposter syndrome would have assumed that I knew what imposter syndrome was. I never had imposter syndrome because I was blissfully unaware that I didn't belong and was just myself. People become anthropologists because they are socially awkward and don't know how to read social situations, but for me, I learned how to read all the mores and rules, though they were stupid, and refused to pay any attention to them anyway. Call it resistance to tyranny or just to shitheads. I think I've always had some sort of eccentric privilege in that people dismiss some of my impolitic behaviors because of who I am and what I bring to the table.

In the Spring, I went with a woman that I was dating to a music festival in East Tennessee called Camp Reggae. The setting was truly amazing. Nestled in bumfuck Egypt, the owners of the property, the Natty Lovejoys built a stage centered in a natural amphitheater. The hallucinogens were plentiful, as was yoga and superb organic food. I tried to spend time with my friend, Margaret, but she seemed more intent on flirting with all the other guys in the camp, which was fine with me because I thought her over-the-top, privileged hippyness was a little much. I spent my time reading Herman Hesse and briefly chatting with one of the band members about the book. Somehow I managed to strike up a friendship with a tall, red dreadlocked woman named Jessica. We ate mushrooms and explored the surrounding land, at one point becoming engulfed in the sound of frogs groaning in the olive green pond. It was a profoundly beautiful experience and freeing after the years of emotional manipulation and abuse by Sarah.

Jessica was a Montessori teacher in Knoxville, kind and gentle, though the yoga instructor seemed to take some offense at our friendship. He was overtly hostile. How yogic.

My mental health was deteriorating. I was experimenting with hallucinogens, especially mushrooms, and struggling to deal with the fact that within academia, I was "special." Academic legitimacy is as much about who you are as what you do.

Personality, especially among young professors, matters more than intelligence or accomplishments, until it doesn't. My Southern working class disposition, combined gifts and the recognition of the faculty at Auburn was strange for me to handle. Less than two years earlier I was an anonymous redneck doing pretty well in school and now I was known on campus as a rising scholar with rumors that I was going to Ivy League caliber school.

The most difficult part of my success was feeling a huge burden to represent my entire state and the working people in it at some strange university that thought I was "unique." The burden was overwhelming because no one in the South is under any illusions about what the rest of the country thinks of us. Redneck jokes are politically correct and I've been in an academic conference where the speaker used the term "poor white trash." A future mentor did correct the speaker during Q&A, which won my immediate respect.

The anxieties about not coming off as a stereotype, of representing my people, and my deteriorating mental health combined with self-medication through alcohol and marijuana led to many dark nights, delusional thinking especially of the grandiose type, and deep sadness and regret for the tragedy of our species and that I was somehow out here as its savior. I was obsessed with social movements to an unhealthy point. I was reading about social movements from all over the world and found myself drawn to the Zapatista Movement. The media savvy and proficiency with using global activist networks struck me as a novel and effective way to get attention to some remote part of the world such as Birmingham. But, I saw myself as a leader and revelled in the thoughts of glory and transformation. I even told someone that I wanted to lead a violent revolution, which was both grandiose and a testament to my mental health at the time. I think folks just thought that I was eccentric, but there was more to it than that.

The summer after I did the Sand Mountain research was one of the best moments of my life. I had started dating a woman from Mobile named Alyson in a relationship that was fiery and beautiful but would burn out fast. I also did an internship with Alabama Sustainable Agriculture Network in what I am now sure was an interview for executive director. Many folks inquired suspiciously if I was going to stick around. I told them that I didn't know. It also introduced me to development for the first time when I worked alongside Andrew, a longtime Natural Resource Conservation Service agent. We did a few things with farmers but I was concerned with other stuff, like dealing with my growing madness.

Alyson was incredible for me. I hadn't been in a real relationship since my divorce and was more than a little bitter. But, she was patient and appreciated me in a way no woman ever had. We traveled the whole summer in my 1986 Toyota 4Runner which had a removable top, perfect for summer road trips. The funniest trip was when we visited Jason and Bryan in Huntsville. We went to Jason's farm, moved a boat shed on a flatbed trailer, and shot cans and bottles with shot guns. The look on this liberal arts college student with a PhD mom's face during this adventure was priceless. It was a mix of curiosity, shock, and profound horror and when a couple of my friends had a casually sexist conversation in front of her, her feminist sensibilities got to her and she went and cried in the other room. We had a long talk about it on the ride back home and I basically said, "I understand why you are upset, and I'm not justifying what was said, but these are simple, working class people; it's all they know." I don't know exactly how she walked around feeling about it, but it does show the problems with oppressed folks.

We all want to romanticize them as perfect freedom fighters, but the fact is that none of them, none of us, are what we want to see or think should be.

I think we burned out because of my copious drinking and general insanity. The worst part of our short relationship was my bad behavior, particularly the alcohol. Alyson would take me to parties with her friends and I would just drink until I threw up. I was struggling with my identity and an overall malaise. Nothing made sense. Why was an auto mechanic from Huntsville, Alabama going to Berkeley or wherever (I hadn't been accepted yet, but it was a foregone conclusion)? Why did I have to have this burden? What if I just quit and went back to fixing cars? My parents had taught me that my self-worth was based on my intelligence and, as anyone from graduate school will tell you, it becomes that again once you get there. I was confused, upset, and scared, but at the same time enjoying a time in my life when things were remarkably simple.

The work at ASAN was fun and interesting, but I was reading about urbanization and urban development, becoming less and less interested in rural agriculture. I was becoming more of a modern Marxist, though I loved, inexplicably, A Thousand Plateaus by Deleuze and Guattari.

While with Alabama Sustainable Agriculture Network, I did some work for them on one of their prize farms south of Auburn, where I was in school. The farm was run by Christian, deeply Southern farmers. They raised goats. One of their customers was an Islamic family who wanted to buy goats, but wanted to slaughter them themselves in Halal tradition (is that how you say that). The Southern Christian farmers remarked that it was the most humane way that they've ever seen an animal killed (if that can be humane). Western culture doesn't value life the same way that other cultures do. Everything is a puzzle to be solved, pragmatic and material.

The education about culture and people that began right after high school continued unabated throughout college. It wasn't as much rooted in redneck culture's live and let live sensibility at this time, as in social theory. I was losing the redneck and becoming a bourgeois intellectual, which was quite uncomfortable and confusing. It would take years to reconnect with these roots, but abandoning them and even hating them made me unhappy and depressed.

At the end of the summer, Patrick, another friend, and I week to Tuskegee National Forest and ate psilocybin mushrooms. The experience was, by far, the most terrifying experience of my life. I had visions of aliens on trading routes, profound despair, and violent hallucinations. I felt drawn to picking up the axe and chopping my friends to pieces or wandering out in the woods and dying of starvation. While mushrooms are dangerous, it was more than that. I was not completely in control of my faculties and the trajectory of my life supported this. Something was wrong with me.

My political philosophy grew from a critique of the American Dream spurred by Hunter S. Thompson to more Marxist with an interest in social movements. I was fascinated by the Zapatistas, especially the sensationalism and the use of Global North Media. I was beginning to understand some of the basic debates such as the difference between postmodernism and materialist approaches. I was also becoming aware of how working class power is inhibited by race, though my ideas were quite basic.

My radicalism paralleled the development of my madness. The thing about madness is that it gives the mad an insight into the workings of the world both because of the position of mad people on the margins of society and because our brains and spirit don't work in a typical way. We see all the pain and beauty of the world and experience them intensely, emotions that are at once invigorating and profoundly frightening. My life had never been stable. I'd jumped from job to job and friend to friend and woman to woman; nothing had been consistent except maybe abuse from loved ones, which, in and of itself, often leads to altered brain chemistry and madness. I can remember numerous occasions, aided by various mind altering substances, bursting into tears at the thought of any form of oppression and a deeply tortured relationship to the human species, itself seemingly bipolar, capable of both the most unbelievable evil and beauty even in the same action. But, what I always returned to was not particularly that injustice was morally wrong, but that it was fundamentally unnecessary. Nothing is gained through coercion of other living beings, human and the rest. As rednecks often say when spending a boatload of money, you can't take it with you.

I got accepted to Berkeley in the Department of Environmental Science, Policy, and Management in the Spring of 2008 when the most historic presidential election was just getting started. I accepted when Carolyn Finney, a black feminist professor at ESPM, called me. When I received the call, I was playing FIFA soccer with two good ole boys who I worked on four wheel drive trucks with, Lee and Justin, at a trailer that they rented. I accepted entrance into Berkeley while standing on the porch of a trailer where neoconfederate ideology and the n-word were common place. The distance between Carolyn and myself was more than mileage.

The level of confusion associated with going to Berkeley, coupled with my deteriorating mental health made an already difficult transition especially trying. I was going to study with a black woman, but I couldn't help be ashamed of my people's violence toward black people in the South and of my own transgressions as a younger man. I feared going to a place where I knew my accent and even my dress would set me apart from everyone else and would always wonder if people saw me as an ignorant racist simply because who I was and where I was from. This set in motion a long relationship with redneck self-hate and loathing of my people and our history and would take years to overcome. As I would later learn, there's no place for rednecks in academia, especially not redneck political radicals.

I received an internship with Appalachian Sustainable Agriculture Project in Asheville, North Carolina where my anthropology commiserator, drinking and tailgating buddy Debbie was living with her iron pumping boyfriend Jason. The job and the city were great. I basically just researched ag policy at ASAP and spent my time hanging out with radicals that had invaded the city. It was the only place in the world where you can meet a Black Panther and a Klansman at the bus station in the same week. I spent my time going to all manner of events and acting like I knew everything and was everything. I even insulted Julia Butterfly Hill of tree sitting fame. I basically told her in the most unkind and ungenerous way that she was a racist.

This was my first attempt at activism outside of a college campus. New activists, and I was not immune to this, generally think that they know everything and that the reason that the world is not just is because nobody else knows what they're doing. There's quite a bit of this within all activist circles, and it does get to people, but it's especially pronounced among new activists. I pretty much went around telling everyone that they were racist and challenging all of the experienced activists, not accomplishing much but making people annoyed. But, activism and organizing are things that people learn by doing. Reading books like *Rules for Radicals* without an organizing context is like new poker players reading Doyle Brunson's book. You come out thinking that you know all the strategies and tactics, but you basically just piss people off and have no idea what you're talking about. I was this person. Certainly, it would be helpful if elders recognized this dynamic and aided young activists through this phase instead of just going around and bad mouthing them.

Debbie and I would have dated had the situation been different. I met her right after I separated from Sarah and we had a similar penchant for causing trouble in the true redneck tradition. The chemistry between the two of us obviously got under Jerome's skin, and his constant shit talking about everyone, especially gay people, pissed me the fuck off. His no good, trash drug dealer friends made me uncomfortable - that was something that I had put behind me.

Everything came to a head sometime in early July. We were supposed to all meet at a restaurant. Debbie warned me that he was going to confront me and he certainly did. He insulted just about everything about me, but it mostly boiled down to "you think you're so smart." I told him that we should work it out. He threw a glass of water in my face and left.

Internalized oppression. I know we're used to talking about this about people of color but it applies to rednecks too. The problem with Jason wasn't that I thought I was smart, which I most certainly was and am, but that Jason had been told his entire life, by media and culture, that he was stupid. There are only so many times that the Academy or the Library of Congress can recognize Deliverance(s) without starting to believe it just a little bit.

The effect of media and culture on redneck consciousness is to tell us both that we are the true Americans through our hard work, and, subsequently, to tell us that our oppression and poverty are caused by our cultural shortcomings. It's to tell us that we are the superior race and then to demean us when we repeat what has been told to us. Like my father and my first wife, both of whom are white, working class Southerners, the American nation abuses and manipulates us, telling us that we are both occident and orient, but mostly it just tells us to stay in our place. Head down. Work hard. Be thankful for what you have. Don't complain too much. These are redneck values. They clearly don't serve us well.

Debbie told me to leave and I went to live in an anarchist commune that I had previously visited. While I only stayed there for three weeks, it made a profound impression on me. It was organized around the concept of Hakim Bey's Pirate Utopia and was basically what I would later learn was a autonomist commune. There were a lot of drugs, especially hallucinogens, a few live acts, and little money. But, somehow, it more or less worked. Folks were highly independent, but worked collectively to make sure the place ran ok. Doug was the clear charismatic leader and he lived there with his girlfriend. They all dressed like pirates or wenches and quoted Hakim Bey like he was God (I would later learn that Hakim Bey was a favorite of Moorish Black Nationalism and that many of the Black Nationalists didn't know he was white). I struggled with it. The drugs and the constant surveillance by the cops fueled my growing paranoia and the collective style of life was difficult for me to adjust to.

To this day, Asheville, North Carolina is my favorite place that I've ever lived. It's a small town of 70,000 people, but it has a big city, cosmopolitan feel with a beautiful and unique arts and music culture and activism that rivals anywhere in the world. The robust anti-authoritarian, bordering on anarchist, culture, rooted both in Southern culture and leftist politics, felt like home to me. There was no pressure associated with the thickness of reactionary anarchism in Alabama, but an openness that seemed as natural as the majestic Smokies that ringed the city. Even the dominance of Subaru Outbacks, preferred by crusty liberals in the region for their four-wheel drive and large cargo bay, while somewhat humorous and ridiculous, gave the city a warm charm. I want to retire to the hinterland of Asheville and raise goats.

Asheville is what the South could be - deeply anti-authoritarian and dedicated to democracy. Since my time there, it has been discovered by celebrities and faced more than a few gentrification pressures.

In August, I took a bus to Birmingham, broken and hurting, and prepared to start graduate school.

SCHOLAR

My redneckness filled me with anxiety as I embarked on my trip to the left coast. Would people think that I was stupid? Would they think I was a racist? Could I explain myself clearly without resorting to Southern colloquialisms that so colored my language? If one of these colloquialisms came out, would I be perceived as either some character out of Deliverance or some magical intelligent being that talks funny?

I got off the BART with my bags, headed to a Peet's Coffee, where I ordered one small coffee and the clerk said, "one smawwlll cawfee" coming right up. Well, that didn't take long. There were literally thousands of these types of sleights during my time at Berkeley including one where I expressed my frustration working on a project with some of the other students. One of my professors, who was Native American, said, "maybe you shouldn't wear plaid shirts; clothes and accent matter." I have not worn a plaid shirt since then.

But, every time one of these sleights happened, I just thought to myself, "I'm a PHD student at the #1 public university in the world." That helped a lot.

I loved Berkeley. Culture in the South is like the weather - it's dank, hot, and will leave you feeling miserable and not knowing why. In the Bay Area, everything was just chill. Walking down Telegraph was like going to a meeting at the UN with everyone you pass speaking a different language and having a different style of dress. For a curious and somewhat sheltered redneck who only knew two languages - English and Bad English - the initial experience was both terrifying and exhilarating.

The Department of Environmental Science, Policy, and Management where I would spend the next four years was eye opening. There were people from all over the world working on exciting projects and engaging in always innovative and sometimes quite risky research. I struck up a friendship with a hippy intellectual, Paul. On the welcoming camping trip somewhere up in Northern California, Paul and I struck up a conversation about Peter Kropotkin and his arguments about cooperation in nature. It sort of set my mind at ease to have someone to talk with when it was painfully obvious to me that I was the odd duck. I would get used to this odd duck status in the activist and academic spaces that I would inhabit in the coming years. I learned very quickly that I would have to overcome my cultural and geographic handicap with almost anyone who considered themselves a radical of any sort. With socialists my theory wasn't Lenin enough and with intersectionals, the only thing that counts is my racial and gender advantages, though there was a span of time that I mimicked white advocates of intersectionality, especially Tim Wise. More on him later. I don't really know why - it just seemed like an interesting experiment. But neither really work, not because of their content, but because there's no room for disagreement - it's all dogma. (I do seem to get along well with Black Nationalists, go figure). I've never been one to think there's only one way to skin a cat.

I was living with a friend of my brother, Cynthia, and her boyfriend, Toby in a gentrifying area of South Berkeley next to Berkeley Bowl and Ashby BART. My brother and family lived in Richmond, north of Berkeley. My class load was pretty simple, but I was especially excited about taking Advanced Political Ecology, which I had been reading vigorously over the past couple of years.

Political Ecology a discipline focused on the politics of nature, on how nature was created and mediated by living beings. What I liked about it was that it very intentionally included humans in nature as active participants in ecology. This was writing against Cartesian dualism of society and nature.

While I was in a much better place than at the end of the summer, my mental health was clearly deteriorating. I was convinced that one of my professors was out to get me and I wrote my entire paper, citations and all, in about 7 hours between 12 and 7 am. After writing the paper, I played Xbox constantly for the next month and a half, driving my roommates insane. I was reading two books a week and could easily read them in one sitting a piece. I was visiting my brother regularly, obsessed with starting a social movement in Birmingham. The obsession, the energy all symptoms of my growing madness. Needless to say, during this time I was feeling great.

Over the holidays, I started to feel tense. My parents stayed at my brother and sister-in-law's house and it was crowded. I blamed my tension on this.

Classes started back in the Spring of 2009, and I was taking a class on Marx's Capital and a class on race. I was also visiting my brother regularly and still obsessed with starting a social movement in Birmingham. The second or third week of the race class, we had an article on a group of neoconfederates in New Mexico. The article discounted everything they said and seemed to suggest that they shouldn't even be allowed to ranch. My response paper argued that the article was not objective and dismissed everything about the ranchers because of their politics. Another of the response papers argued basically, "who cares about those rednecks?" I was both unprepared for this and coming unglued psychologically.

The next week one of my classmates said that I showed up my professor, Carolyn Finney. I left in the middle of class, went home, deleted all my social media and all my email addresses, and bought plane tickets to Asheville. As soon as I did all this, I realized how insane it was and called my brother to come and get me. The next couple of days are kinda a blur, but I do remember at least two trips to the Tang Center, the UCB medical center, lots of questions about whether I was going to off myself. One thing that I do remember vividly was that I told one of the counselors that my name meant "God is with us." During lunch I realized that my name means "God has remembered." I recognized that I was delusional and was very afraid that I was schizophrenic. My brother and I went back to the Tang Center and I was given an appointment with a psychiatrist. It was there that my life changed profoundly; I was diagnosed with bipolar disorder.

My family and I reached the decision to leave school to recuperate and adjust. They put me on lithium as a mood stabilizer and risperidone, an antipsychotic. The first time I took risperidone it felt like a 100 ton weight was lifted off my shoulders. I spent the next 8 months recuperating in Birmingham in a very low stress environment. I grew a garden with my uncle and worked at West End Community Garden in Birmingham, but mostly I watched NCIS and House reruns trying to come to terms with living with a condition that is not all bad, but does make life more difficult. Truth is, everyone in my family including myself was more than a little relieved. That the condition was treatable gave us all hope that my tumultuous life to this point would balance out. When I called my mom after my meltdown, she said something to the effect of "well, at least you tried." I was thirty years old, had never had a job for more than two years, had never had a relationship more than three, and at least one friend, Bryan, told me that I was going to end up like Rob, who committed suicide. I read a number of books about bipolar disorder and became aware about the connection between bipolar and creativity. I never really thought of myself as a creative person, but looking back on my life, it was clear that creativity was a part of it. I would begin to nurture this, especially in my writing.

In May, I won a National Science Foundation Graduate Research Fellowship, given to the top ten percent of applicants, and decided to return to Berkeley in the fall. I changed the location of my research to Birmingham to work with West End Community Gardens. My obsession with starting a social movement had not subsided.

Having bipolar is being convinced that I'm the smartest person in the world and that I'm destined for greatness and at the same time hating yourself for having knowledge that supposedly no one else knows. This was especially difficult when all hard evidence pointed to the fact that I was brilliant, making distinguishing fact from delusion incredibly hard. It's like telling me that my delusions were accurate. For the longest time, I just outright rejected my intelligence - I just said that it was because I worked harder than everyone else - culturally appropriate for Protestant Southernness and an easy coping mechanism. One day I would have to face this.

Returning to Berkeley was an adventure to say the least. I locked myself out three times in the first week, once scaling to the second floor to climb in through a window, and once kicking the door in with my boot.

But, I survived. The next four years would be years of solitude, meditation, and the development of my political theory. I was living in a dumpy room in a rooming house about three blocks from campus. I was taking three classes - race and environment, Gramsci and community development. The professor of the Gramsci class clearly didn't want me in the class, and though I learned a lot, most of the students were pretty hostile to me because I didn't know all the cool socialist theories. Funny that the only working class person in the class was not good enough for a class on working class liberation. I did love Gramsci, though, and would use his ideas in my later organizing and activism. Gramsci brought culture into Marxism and as an anthropologist, I understood the power of culture. I wanted to use his ideas to leverage Southern culture for liberation. That's what this memoir is about.

During this time, I was dating a woman named Ashley, a ridiculously wealthy, country song-writer who I met at Hardly Strictly Bluegrass, a yearly free bluegrass festival in Golden Gate Park, when she offered me a hit of her pipe (I didn't partake). We both had bipolar disorder and I spent a lot of time traveling back and forth to her huge house because she lived in the Palo Alto area. I got the distinct impression that she wanted a Southerner on her arm to show off to all her country music friends. The last time I spoke with her, she invited me to go to Chicago with her to a concert. She would pay for all of it. I declined and I have often wondered what my life would have been like had I ditched class and been her arm candy.

I came to Berkeley wanting to learn about social movements. Much of the books that I had read on social movements were based on rational-choice theory, which didn't seem to be a deep dive into the mechanics of movements. These theories basically said that social movements were marketing phenomena and didn't really go into popular education or even the mechanics of change.

Movements, to these theories, were basically about getting money and advertising. I wouldn't necessarily find what I was looking for until I was more involved in movements, but I was developing a robust analysis of what was going on and how social problems came to be. Essentially, my graduate education would be the creation of my own theory of what was wrong. Only the last chapter in my dissertation would scrape the surface of how to address these problems.

Coming into grad school, I understood the basics. I understood that there was materialist theory, the idea that what we do creates reality, and idealist theory, the concept that what we think creates reality. While neither of these approaches is wrong per se, and both have strengths and weakness, I tended toward materialism because, as a former working class person, I recognized that we all learn from doing and develop ideas in relationship to what we are doing. There was one problem with this - race, which I had come to Berkeley to learn more about because it seemed pivotal to creating a new movement in Alabama, was strictly in the idealist camp.

Critical race theory was the most accepted way to deal with race within academia. It held that racism was, in fact, normal and that all institutions operated based in one way or the other on institutional cultures of white supremacy. This meant that all people had mostly non-conscious ideas of racial superiority and inferiority in their head and that people's normal behaviors were all tinged with racial bias. Clearly, according to this theory, white supremacy and racism were the results of the ideas, even non-conscious ones, in people's heads that dictated their behavior. Critical race theory leads to a number of different types of approaches to dealing with race including trauma, internalized racial oppression, media analysis, but what I was interested in was white privilege theory.

Personally, white privilege theory was a little difficult for me to swallow at first. My life had taken a circuitous road and there were times in my life where I could see little institutional privilege. Often, white privilege is looked at somewhat narrowly and absent of any true intersectional analysis, seemingly directed at liberal whites to get them to recognize that their nominal anti-racism isn't enough. However, as a working class white, much of the analysis seemed only tangentially true. I struggled to make it apply to my life, but I was, nonetheless, interested in ways to apply it more meaningfully.

On the materialist side, I was in fucking theory heaven. Lefebvre and David Harvey's analysis of urban space stuck like glue. I could walk around Berkeley or any city for that matter and question why buildings were where they were, why people engaged in the behaviors that they were engaged in, and how space was arranged in such a way as to facilitate making gobs and gobs of money. Harvey's Limits to Capital is probably one of the most important books that I've ever read, a detailed analysis of every single conceivable thing about late capitalism. It spoke to me more than critical race theory because I could clearly see myself in the analysis, while critical race theory often has the unfortunate quality of homogenizing people of different races in a way that materialism does not. I believe that this is done for the sake of analysis, a necessary abstraction to elucidate an analysis, but I often wonder, when operationalized and relying solely on idealism, if it does more harm than good. The great thing about materialist dialectics is that the window is practice, which can be easily recorded, along with people's interpretation of those practices, while idealist analysis relies all too heavily on guessing what is in people's head, and what's more, what's in people's head that they don't know is there.

You can see what people do and that's what makes materialist analysis superior.

Yet, I struggled mightily with integrating the two types of approaches and since little materialist race approaches exist, I decided that I was going to develop a materialist theory of race that would open up space for the potential of a class-based, multiracial movement around material realities.

During this time, I was also developing methodological chops. Being interested in social movements, I was naturally drawn to participatory action research, a method designed involve the researched in the process of knowledge creation. PAR owes its existence to people like Paulo Freire and Myles Horton, so I spent my time studying Pedagogy of the Oppressed, Freire's book and Highlander Research and Education Center, becoming an adoring fanboy of the latter. These folks understood oppressed people. They understood the legions of well-meaning saviors and developmentalists who came into oppressed communities such as peasant communities in Brazil, where Freire worked, and the rednecks in Appalachia, where Horton worked, who often had no idea how to work with oppressed people and were unintentionally condescending and patronizing, often doing much more harm than good. Freire and Horton understood that the oppressed have to do for themselves, discover their own solutions, and contemplate their own role and place in the universe, and that it was the educator's place to show the oppressed the door to a world of potential and freedom, not impose knowledge designed to facilitate oppression.

I also came to know method by another if related meaning - thinking about thinking - and began to understand the dialectical method, particularly in the context of community work. Freire was obviously steeped in Marxist theory, and his book was about liberatory dialectical education. So, I began to think of community work as a dialogue between me, a bourgeois academic (for now), and the community in a process in which we both internalized the knowledge of the other creating a learning community. And this is what popular education is all about - creating flat, learning communities where knowledge creation reflects everyone's unique talents.

This time was a time of meditation and self-reflection and I spent much of my time alone. I did have a few friends, though. Liviu was an exchange student from Germany and a peasant from

Romania. He was a misogynist, an anti-semite, and a puckish

asshole, but he reminded me of my friends from Alabama and we

liked similar heavy metal music. He seemed to love the sound of his

own voice and would talk incessantly in Louise's class, who was one

of my mentors. There were only two men in the class and I'm pretty

sure all the women except Genevieve hated him and with good

reason. Genevieve also became one of my friends and would be the

co-author on a paper we published in Urban Geography in 2014.

The three of us would rent a car and travel to Yosemite one weekend

with two of Genevieve's friends from Spain. The five of us

crammed into a small Chevy and drove out there.

Like much of my experience in Berkeley, the trip was an

education in cross-cultural interaction. The two Spanish women

didn't speak English, but Liviu and Genevieve did, so in half the

conversations, I had no idea what was going on. The Europeans

were fucking fascinated with American fast food and seemed to have

no sense of time, while Genevieve and I tried to hurry them along to

get to our destination, where we arrived at like 11 pm and bogarted

someone else's camp site. Liviu grilled some cheap ribs, sang some

Romanian drinking songs, and saw a bear in the camp licking the grease from the ribs. I sang Amazing Grace and the Spanish women were mesmerized. Learning to live and let live is something not taught in the South, but I learned it during my time of solitude in California.

I spent many nights with Liviu, drinking beer and arguing about theory. I even smoked a little weed with him, but it made me super paranoid and Liviu tried to calm me down. One of our last experiences before he went back to Germany was to watch the Auburn vs. Alabama game at a local bar called Raleigh's. Liviu and I both loved Raleigh's because they had a bunch of beers and good chicken wings, the latter of which he fell in love with. Auburn was losing 24-0 at halftime and I was already drunk. The team came back, led by the immortal Cam Newton, to win 28-27 and by the end of the game everyone in the bar was pulling for Auburn. During this, Liviu went outside and smoked weed and got busted by the cops, but they let him go with basically a ticket. I will never forget this experience my entire life - trying to explain football to Liviu and Auburn winning one of the most legendary games in school history on the way to winning one of our two national championships.

I'm still friends with Genevieve to this day and she was an important part of my experience on the West Coast. Every time we would meet, we would alternate going to a Spanish place where I could eat meat, and going to a vegan place for her. She would always get mad at me for drinking too much and I would always take the BART home late at night, drunker than Cooter Brown and stumble up the hill in Berkeley to my home. She always took me to this multi-cultural art crawl that was always packed out, but super cool. She also did all the GIS work on our paper.

My meditations and experiences were all swirling in my head. I began looking at Birmingham by studying segregation statistics, as Birmingham is the most segregated metro area in the South. My local knowledge of the area told me that blacks and whites lived in almost different worlds and the segregation statistics supported this fact. I became curious as to how this isolation shaped the consciousness of black and white people in Birmingham, a question shaped by reading Bourdieu. Bourdieu argued that the social structures in the world also shaped how we act in the world and how we understand those actions. While Bourdieu was talking about class cultures, I began trying to adapt his ideas to race, and in

Birmingham, white supremacist social structures clearly have a spatial correlate. This budding understanding of the materialist aspects of race would be the theory that I would bring with me to the field.

I began my dissertation research the following summer studying a coalition of 25 organizations that received stimulus money to create a food policy council.

West End Community Garden was and is a program of Urban Ministry. The director, Ama, was the go to black woman in the food movement, a movement dominated by mostly white organizations and institutions including Main Street Birmingham, which would later become REV, Jones Valley Urban Farm, the brain child of Edwin Marty, Magic City Harvest, and the Jefferson County Department of Health. The meetings were starkly homogenous - white professionals with a profound inability to connect in any way with even the black leaders of Birmingham, much less grassroots activists. A stream of so called experts gave advice at each and every meeting about how to market and sell in the local food system to what was basically a middle class white audience. People repeated that we must be careful with the "messaging," which was a thinly veiled phrase that meant attempting to market to people in the suburbs with money who are conservative and almost exclusively white. There were no black community or religious leaders present at any of the meetings. I'm pretty sure that they had no idea that it was going on. Ama spoke for "the community," a euphemism for black people, even though I doubt that she wanted that role. The big thing that they wanted to do is create a food policy council to get ordinances passed in the metro area.

The whole process was a shit show. Every group in the coalition was looking out for number one and there was no one talented enough with people to forge consensus. I wrote a letter after I returned to Berkeley criticizing the group for lack of diversity and got absolutely no response and the November Food Summit proved to be a ridiculous exercise in self-gratification and a lesson on how exclusively white conceptualized and implemented programs have no chance of success.

There were too many problems to get deep into what happened with the grant, but segregation played a major role. The people involved, though many of them were involved with charity organizations that served black people, hadn't the slightest idea what black people experience in this city. The solutions that they floated were so tone deaf and ridiculous that it seemed impossible that educated people would actually think they were good ideas. An idea that was seriously floated was to get Kobe Bryant to market fresh produce to poor black people. The level of racism and absurdity was beyond the pale.

It's hard to say that it was even a movement. Nobody was involved but well-paid professionals. There was no mention of community organizing at all or of going to neighborhood meetings to get black folks involved. In fact, the United Way, which played a pivotal role in this mess, never mentioned community organizing until 2016, six years from when I suggested it. Combine this with an utter lack of leadership and organization and just about all of the $6.5 million went to waste.

To illustrate this, a respected neighborhood leader and president of the citizens advisory board, Sheila Tyson, a black community leader, told an organizer of the Food Summit that Tyson was needed for this group to accomplish anything, which was absolutely true. The Food Summit organizer then went around and told everyone that Tyson was crazy, parroting the white narrative about her. White people love to talk shit about Tyson because she talks different than the way white folks, especially professionals talk. She doesn't use sterile, sanitized language that white people deem appropriate and she talks openly about race, poverty, and oppression, which whites have successfully rendered unacceptable in any real way. It's totally acceptable to talk about poor people in terms of giving them shit, but to speak of oppression or racism existing, much less fighting it, will get you written out of the will, and since whites have all the money, whites are able to dictate the terms of the talk. The few black people who do get to participate know full well what to say and what not to say. And yet, nothing works right in Birmingham because white professionals design, create, and implement programs that have no fucking chance of helping black folks or the poor. Everything in Birmingham must be approved by wealthy whites before it gets done. They hold the doors and the gates, and, almost without fail, never do anything that helps, but they have no reservations about using Birmingham as an ATM machine.

So basically, you have wealthy whites who control everything, middle class whites with resources who try to help but have no idea how to, black leaders who have to capitulate to both groups of whites or be denied everything, and poor black people who are just screwed. It's not a pretty picture, and combine it with the seemingly deliberate intransigence of every white dominated institution in Birmingham and Birmingham probably hasn't had anything meaningful done for the 31% in poverty since the end of the Civil Rights Movement, which many, many community leaders feel like was a pyrrhic victory.

My instincts were correct that segregation contributed greatly to Birmingham's dysfunction. Birmingham's race discourse, at least at this time, was basically like Race Fight Club. The first rule is that you don't talk about it, mostly because it's impolite. If you do talk about it, make sure no one is offended and definitely don't call out respected leaders no matter how obvious it is. Segregation is Birmingham is deep, deeper than just geography, and extending to culture, politics, family, gender, and much more. In Birmingham, there are two of everything - a black and a white - and the only thing that we really agree on is that we love football. My little letter to the grantees and my subsequent activism has black-balled me from any participation in any of the well-funded non-profits and locked me out of the political class, so much so that our later strategy would be to bypass Birmingham's institutions completely, and look at regional and national networks.

The grant ultimately failed and did not produce one deliverable.

Yet, there was a growing subterranean movement of discontent within the city. A few black nationalists were starting to organize by going to public housing and talking to the residents. Most of these folks were marginally employed, excluded from the system, but passionate and intelligent. Many were talented poets and were showing up at local rallies doing confrontational verse. Much of this was poorly organized and haphazard, but it did show that there were people, on the fringes, that recognized what was going on and how important it would be to respond.

Before I returned to Berkeley, I met a woman at a local foods meeting at Grow Alabama run by Jerry Spencer. Spencer had a reputation, deserved or not, as a sort of local foods huckster and had been accused of using the organic label on conventional produce. I began talking with this woman, Robyn, who seemed quite confident and sure of herself. We discussed the local food movement and the food summit and became so engrossed in conversation that Spencer had to tell us to shut up because he was talking. I was intrigued by this woman, who is now my wife and God bless her for it. I'm obviously not easy.

In November, Robyn wrote me an email inviting me to the Food Summit. I bought plane tickets and left for Birmingham the next Friday. I got to spend some time with Robyn at the Food Summit, which she was helping to organize, and on Saturday we met at West End Community Garden. In a debate that rages to this day, it is still a point of discussion as to who was chasing who, but both Myron, the farm manager, and my dad, specifically pointed out that she was chasing me. Only history will tell.

ORGANIZER

Our first date was December 17, 2010. We went to a now closed, shitty sushi restaurant in Hoover, a suburb of Birmingham and then to a Birmingham institution, The Nick, for a little dancing and drinking. I told her I was a feminist and I think she fell in love. I made a joke about Lord of the Rings and she was entranced. Halfway through the set, she said "you gonna kiss me now?" and I was in love. We watched the Auburn vs Oregon national championship game with my dad and I think she thought we were crazy, but Auburn won. I went back to Berkeley, returning in the summer to do my dissertation research. She was and is an entrancing woman. Kind, passionate, loving, and just enough of a bitch to keep me on my toes. We kept in touch over Skype while I was at Berkeley and I knew that I wanted to spend my life with her.

My study of the food movement, broader analysis of Birmingham in general, and discussions with a few black leaders had me thinking about creating an organization. It was the summer of 2011. I had prepared a plan to work with my community partners, West End Community Garden, and they flatly refused. I had to find a new community to work with to do my research and I contacted Virginia Ward, who worked doing urban agriculture in Western Jefferson County. It was also becoming clear that most organizations were either underfunded or controlled by whites or political patronage, which at the end of the day meant basically the same thing. Whites control Birmingham politics. I was also working with a woman named Anna, who was a University of Alabama, Birmingham graduate student.

With another woman, Virginia Ward, a community leader in the Grasselli Neighborhood, we created Magic City Agriculture Project. The earliest iterations of this consisted on Anna and I working on various farms throughout Birmingham and creating what was essentially an anti-racist book club. The movement that I wanted to start was beginning. I was engaging online about race, using Social Justice Warrior tactics and attempting to put what I was learning through my dissertation research into some sort of practice. I had a small reputation as a shit starter and bomb thrower and I would go right back at folks who insulted me, which was more than a little ill-advised.

We also worked with Virginia on Southwest Birmingham Community Farm, a new project of Project Hopewell, the non-profit arm of Hopewell Missionary Baptist Church. Main Street Birmingham, a well-funded and connected economic development organization, was beginning a partnership with Project Hopewell to create farmers' markets in the neighborhood.

Project Hopewell assembled neighborhood and religious leaders and Sam Crawford and Taylor Clark gave a very slick presentation about how farmers' markets would alleviate hunger, a dubious claim at best. Main Street Birmingham had been central to the food policy council debacle and their top down, parachute in development strategy was foreboding for the project. The first farmers' market was an absolute catastrophe with no one from either organization staffing the market.

Main Street Birmingham called a meeting and proceeded to chew Project Hopewell out like they were a disobedient child. I don't necessarily blame Main Street Birmingham for the miscommunication, but the way they handled it was amateurish at best. The problem could have been solved collectively and it could have worked, but Sam and Taylor blew it up. Project Hopewell pulled out and took a significant hit in reputation with the community and Main Street Birmingham conned some unsuspecting local into heading the market, she quit six weeks later and told me that she felt used. Virginia said that they were "prostituted."

Main Street Birmingham, which would later become REV Birmingham, did a bang up job selling it to everyone else. They held a press conference at the market with the Mayor, William Bell, representatives from the Department of Health, and, of course, Main Street Birmingham. No one from Project Hopewell spoke. They also contracted with ChangeLab Solutions out of Oakland, to create a white paper claiming credit for Main Street and obliquely blaming Hopewell for the failure. The whole thing was a crock of shit.

The reason this failed is simple. Nobody at Main Street Birmingham has any fucking clue how to do community development. It's a bunch of business people that know how to make money and know nothing about people, especially poor and oppressed people.

Part of the prevailing wisdom with Main Street Birmingham and with the food movement, loosely defined, was that all problems can be fixed outside of politics and power. The overarching culture of the entire movement was one of technocrats. Need people to eat healthy food - form a food policy council. Need to address food deserts - put a farmers' market in a poor neighborhood. There is no analysis of the underlying conditions that cause hunger and the dominance of fast food outlets in poor neighborhoods. There's no analysis that obesity may in fact be caused by cortisol associated with the increased stress of being black and poor. There's no deep dive into why grocery stores are unprofitable, but mostly, all of the so-called solutions never include the analysis of the people who actually live there. Nobody asks them what they want to do, and that's why all of this fails. That and the lack of commitment from organizations like Main Street Birmingham to the communities that they serve. They're just trying to meet the reporting requirements for a grant or to the public and then on to the next project. This parachute in type of development is so damaging to poor communities because resources get used, but they never see any benefits from these resources, only a ton of broken promises and empty agreements.

Race plays such a pivotal role in these failures because institutional knowledge tells development organizations that people in poor neighborhoods can't solve their own problems because, if they could, they already would have. So development organizations come in with a bunch of well-meaning, fancy ideas with no root in the conditions of the community and, at the first sign of trouble, throw their hands up and walk away, mumbling to themselves that "these folks don't want help." I have news for all these development organizations - what you're providing ain't help.

I was more or less an observer in all this and really didn't know what I was looking at until much later. I've hesitated to write anything about this anywhere because people at Hopewell fear retaliation. By the time this is published, it will be seven years since this has happened and I think people need to know. After the debacle (the second in a couple of years for the "food movement"), I volunteered to assistant teach the GED class at Hopewell. I'm not sure if I taught anything useful, but, boy, did I get an education.

The problem with a GED class in poor neighborhoods is that a high school diploma is worth virtually nothing and a GED is worth less. The participation is the class was ridiculously inconsistent and the consistent students were only there because it was court ordered, like someone selling drugs because they were poor is going to be that much better off with a GED. I had studied Freirean popular education, but there was no time to actually get students used to bottom up learning and there was definitely a level of comfort with top down oppressive education because most of them had grown up with it. Also, at this point in my life, popular education was more of a theory than a practice and I sucked at it. After three months, I could tell that I wasn't doing a lick of good, though it was eye-opening how shitty these folks' lives were. I got way more of an education than they did.

Still working with Project Hopewell, Incorporated, Magic City Agriculture Project focused on helping PHI with Southwest Birmingham Community Farm even though PHI's expectations for the farm were unrealistic at best and probably impossible. They wanted the whole community to produce food for free during their spare time, time poor folks don't have. The thing about community gardens is that nobody ever wants to work in them unless they get paid, the food ain't enough and successful gardens in disadvantaged neighborhoods have a paid staff, usually heavily subsidized by a non-profit or government entity. The notion that gardens are somehow a productive community space is a great line for donors and foundations but it couldn't be farther from the truth. In contrast, a cooperative production garden, could make a big difference because it creates economic activity, not charity.

MCAP basically ran the garden for four years.

Southwest Birmingham Community Farm itself was cool. It had drip irrigation and a hoop house, both provided by the Tuskegee and the NRCS, and was fairly high tech and productive, but the organizational model could never work and we tried repeatedly to get them to sell the product and organize it into a cooperative, to no avail. It got hit by a tornado in 2015, but was rebuilt and now employs youth interns to run the farm during the summer. MCAP did learn quite a bit about neighborhood and organizational politics throughout the process and even raised $5000 dollars for the farm to buy equipment.

We were adding board members and looking for people to work with. We knew that we wanted to do antiracism and technical assistance to sort of be like a combination of Highlander and the Federation of Southern Cooperatives and we had some vague idea about doing aquaponics cooperatives. I had briefly helped this dude in Richmond, Miguel Espino, with. Aside from that we just bounced around from one wild goose chase to the next. Anna, who is queer, moved to Ithaca, New York I think in part because folks around here, black and white, are so shitty to queer people. Last time I spoke with Anna she was thriving. Good for her.

This was 2012 and I was working on my dissertation for Berkeley, which was going reasonably well. I had this strange idea, inspired by Hunter S. Thompson, about "Gonzo Research" in which researchers go out and create the data for the research. To some degree, I accomplished this with MCAP, but MCAP wasn't fully developed enough to write a whole dissertation about it. I basically wrote the dissertation as a prima facie case for MCAP's existence and to identify where MCAP would work socioculturally, politically and economically.

Over the next year or so, we would work on land bank legislation, which helped us to build a relationship with councilor Sheila Tyson even though she was completely out-maneuvered by the Mayor, a veteran politician. Any negotiation should start with an ask for everything that is possible and even a couple of things that are impossible and Tyson started with compromise. The Mayor got a land bank controlled by community development, which he controlled. He was also on the board.

I interviewed for the board of the Birmingham Land Bank Authority at the request of Tyson. I came in with an idea for the board that would create permanently affordable housing and prefer potential land owners of color for disposition of tax delinquent properties. When I said this, Councilor Abbott, who is a long-standing white city councilor from Southside, needed to pick her jaw up off the table and then subsequently tried to argue that I was "not qualified." I wasn't chosen, and in retrospect, I was never enough of an insider to get that position and Tyson and her Chief of Staff, Kelvin Datcher just wanted to send a message. We would develop a friendship with Datcher who basically ran Tyson's office while she was out in the West End community. Tyson also told everyone that could hear her at a press conference that Rob, our white executive director, was her "future husband."

White people always hated Sheila Tyson. She's country; she's from the streets; and she speaks her mind and white folks, without fail, say that she's unprofessional. Many think that she's crazy and others think that she is stupid. This has less to do with

Tyson and more to do with the fact that most blacks and whites live in different worlds with different styles of communication and different rules for acceptable public behavior. Many middle class blacks don't like Tyson either, which is respectability politics plain and simple. But, Tyson is pure. She speaks for the people, she speaks like them, and she represents them, and I respect her for it, especially in a city this hierarchical and in which both black and white leaders produce this sanitized racial narrative based on a Santa Claus-ification of Martin Luther King, Jr. and to some extent Fred Shuttlesworth to balance rich and poor, black and white, and move the city "forward" whatever that means. Well, it basically means that black and white leaders agree to enrich themselves at the expense of everyone else and Tyson is a fly in this ointment.

We hired Rob, I think in 2012 or 2013, when his wealthy mom agreed to pay his salary. It was not necessarily a favorable agreement, but it did take pressure off of me so that I could work on my dissertation and try to get a job. Rob was a naive young guy with a big heart. He pissed off everyone in the Hopewell community, Hillman Station, within a week of his hiring. He was pretty lost for the first couple of years, but grew into a very effective organizer and activist. On top of this, he also has a terrible degenerative disease called Cystic Fibrosis and spends a lot of time in the hospital.

After a lot of riding around with Anna trying to start gardens and doing a bunch of stuff that didn't make any difference and trying to work with folks who didn't want help, we had a strategy session in March of 2012. Our coalition, which was a grand total of seven people at this time, decided that we would try to change the conversation about Birmingham's economic development by calling it gentrification and we would try to change the discussion about race by using social justice warrior tactics, though we did not call the latter this. I created my first blog on gentrification on Food Justice Politics, and I predicted that Woodlawn, a poor, black community in Eastern Birmingham, would gentrify four years before anyone would mention anything about that community gentrifying. We also started a whisper campaign about REV Birmingham, for both how they communicate with people and their role in promoting gentrification.

I was going to be the public speaker of these ideas along with the target, while others would work quietly behind the scenes and chime in where necessary. We had no money, but we decided to use the media, specifically social media and be opportunistic, especially with panels about development. Our primary target was I Believe in Birmingham, a Facebook group created by Joseph Casper Baker III and also utilizing the connections that I made with Mark Kelly, publisher of Weld, a local weekly newspaper, now defunct and Joseph Bryant, a journalist for The Birmingham News.

People were furious. The culture of I Believe in Birmingham was such that most of the white people their had wrapped their identity around white savior narrative of saving the city and public institutions and private development organizations like REV Birmingham played it up dramatically. I also used very sensational tactics like getting into insult wars with other posters, playing up my education, and basically insulting all of the sacred cows especially of these "believers," as they are called in the secular religion of Birmingham. People hated me in a deep personal way. Reddit threads emerged trashing me and talking about how terrible I was stopping just short of insulting my family. Seasoned local activists thought that I was crazy. But, it gained traction.

In January of 2013, I wrote an article for Weld, Kelly's paper, about gentrification and got a ridiculous rebuttal by Andrew

Wheeler-Berliner that has since been taken down. I don't want to come across like we knew exactly what we were doing. Like most of the stuff we did and would do, we basically figured it out as we went along. People were pissed and arguing about I Believe in Birmingham, referred to as IBIB on thread with 200 and 300 comments much of which were insults on my character was putting gentrification on the map. After my article, Kelly would publish a series of articles investigating gentrification and public opinion was turning. The city was still firmly under the belief that what they were doing subsidizing gentrification was helping, almost unanimously.

In the Spring of 2014, while I was a post-doc at the Southern Foodways Alliance at Ole Miss, Sidewalk, a local independent film non-profit, planned to show My Brooklyn, a film on gentrification, with a panel on gentrification. Rob knew Josh Vasa, one of their employees, and managed to get me on the panel. This would be a pattern - though we brought the gentrification discussion to Birmingham, everyone wants someone from the establishment to comment. We would always have to fight to get me on the panels. This is not so much a slight to us as a statement about the rigidly hierarchical and opaque nature of the Birmingham establishment, which basically enforces indirect rule. Select black folks are chosen to lead, but they are always controlled by suburban whites. They defend the racial and economic balance that supposedly moves the city forward.

We prepared rigorously for the panel. I studied for weeks and we held mock panels at my friend Austin's house. The strategy for the panel was to control the narrative by introducing a new wrinkle to the gentrification discussion, hopefully catching the other panelists unaware. Up to this point, we mostly talked about gentrification as displacement. For this panel, I was going to talk about gentrification not helping the majority of the city. Poverty had risen during the years of gentrification. It worked flawlessly. Kelly, the moderator, introduced the conversation as about displacement and when I gave my opening statement, I talked about poverty. (Kelly literally asked me a question about displacement and I answered a question about poverty, which clearly startled him. Always answer the question that you want asked.) The entire discussion was about poverty ranging from the lack of affordable housing to the lack of food.

There were a lot of murmurs about me on this panel. I put those to rest and Kelly was impressed with "the way I handled myself." Probably the most interesting thing that was said was when a local woman asked what I was doing on the panel when I was a professor at Ole Miss. I said that, "I was born here," but I wished I would have said "do you think I'm a 'outside agitator' or maybe 'agitata,' Bull Connor's favorite phrase, which speaks to the provinciality of the region.

We continued our social media activism pretty consistently and were still working with PHI on their garden.

The next big panel was held by the Birmingham Museum of Art called BMA Speaks: Birmingham's Renaissance. Again, we had to fight to get me on the panel, but Max Rykov relented when we showed him all of the research that I had done. It was in late 2015. By this time, we had many allies among activists and regular folk's opinion of Birmingham's development was changing, including among neighborhood leaders. Neighborhoods consistently felt left behind.

At this point, I had done many panels on both race and gentrification and was pretty seasoned. I knew the strategy was that you basically ignore the moderator's questions and just say whatever you want. We felt like there was a pretty strong understanding of gentrification among the public, something the moderator and organizers dramatically underestimated. Our strategy was to go in and talk about alternatives and how the city was just putting money behind wealthy suburbanites. There was a developer on the panel who opened with some weird discussion about music, which I think was an attempt to humanize him, but he didn't talk the last 1:45 of a 2 hour panel. The fact that a mainstream, establishment organization like the Birmingham Museum of Art would even countenance such as discussion was a huge win.

The watershed moment happened in the Spring of 2016. The Mayor and his buddies in the suburbs and Montgomery crafted a state-wide bill that would cede enormous power to the Mayor. Under indirect rule, this would give colonial establishment 9 less people to control (the city council) in Birmingham. There was a public meeting about this bill and to everyone's surprise, many of the citizens railed against gentrification and white folks moving to the city. This was huge because it wasn't some white academic saying, but regular, everyday folk. Many of the cities leaders went into full panic. John Archibald, probably the most respected journalist in Alabama, said that gentrification wasn't happening, but that the city had failed to support black businesses. Seemed like distinction without difference to me.

Now everybody in the city was talking about gentrification. NPR ran a series of stories on Birmingham's development, calling it uneven. They hosted a live call-in show with Sam Douglas, respected establishment activist, Steven Hoyt, grassroots city councilor, and Brian Wolfe, developer. I was expecting a bunch of hem-hawing and soft pedaling and it started out like that, but, a couple of callers called in railing on gentrification and Hoyt and Douglas opened up. Wolfe even tried to justify gentrification using the word gentrification. Public opinion had changed.
The cherry on top was NPR's use of the term "uneven" to describe gentrification, when that is exactly what Marxist scholars call it. Neil Smith, who wrote the bible on gentrification, The New Urban Frontier, based on this theory of Uneven Development. According to Smith, gentrification was urban uneven development. The idea of NPR unwittingly using Marxist language is beyond hilarious.

We won.

The white privilege campaign didn't go as well. Disaster is the word that comes to mind, though it probably wasn't an unmitigated disaster. The first mistake was adopting Tim Wise's Social Justice Warrior tactic of trying to shame everyone into believing that they have white privilege. Wise is a fairly well known social commentator who uses high levels of sensationalism and confrontation to get his point across. It's great for creating a sensational narrative, but the fact is that NOBODY IS FUCKING LISTENING. Folks just tune out. The other problem with these tactics is that they are dehumanizing. Telling someone that they are privileged erases all of their experiences and reduces all of their experiences to racial experience, which, while technically correct, is a lot more complex than this.

I did this for years and some local activists tried to have interventions with me, but I refused to listen for a long time adding to my emerging brand of insanity. There are probably hundreds of people that I need to apologize to including many mentors who all taught me that community organizing is about relationships and not ideology. It's a terrible tactic and Michael Harriot aptly pointed out that "white allies are really just Caucasian hoteps," which is a hilarious statement. In some ways, I think that it is a phase that antiracist activists go through, but it can only be a phase.

My phase lasted a couple of years, but, ironically, after hanging out with black nationalists and how they approached race and racism, I started rethinking in terms of a spiritual approach to how I am shaped by race and white supremacy and instead of trying to shame people into some sort of quasi-evangelical conversion, the key was to get folks to question who they are and why they are - to set people on a path instead of demand obedience.

The on the ground stuff started in late 2014 with the beginning of the Black Lives Matter-Birmingham movement and their actions. The movement was basically led by Avee-Ashanti Shabazz, a charismatic, highly-intelligent, activist, who has some weird views about women and queer folk, and Mercutio Southall, Sr., a passionate, quasi-anarchic, but highly effective protestor, who became famous for fucking up a Trump rally in Birmingham. MCAP offered to raise money for bail for the group and bailed out Mercutio after he got tazed like 15 times at the Homewood Walmart as he was leaving the protest. Their protests involved announcing on the internet the day of the time and location of the protests, which were mostly attended by white people. I'm not sure what the goal was, but it got all over the media and led to a bunch of arrests. I respect Mercutio and Avee more than just about anyone that I've been involved with in Birmingham because they do the work with no thought of reward and a purity that is rare in the non-profit driven movement world.

By this time, I was transitioning out of leadership at MCAP. Richard Rice, a local lawyer, was going to replace me as board president and I was thinking about my life post MCAP. We were also writing a strategic plan for a cooperative economy in Birmingham. I was also becoming friends with Susan Diane Mitchell and Majadi Baruti and they were becoming team members of MCAP.

I needed to make some money. It became clear that my academic career was not going to happen. I sent in over 200 applications and got two interviews, one at Birmingham Southern College, a Methodist college, for director of the service learning program.

In an interview that will probably go down in history as the worst interview on record, I tried to explain popular education to a marketing professor and a chemist, which was hilariously painful. I had developed a whole program for transforming the Rise3, a service learning program, into an effective community tool and working in the Smithfield neighborhood where MCAP was working. Birmingham Southern wanted a smooth talking corporate shill to sell the program to donors and the rest of the university. They said that they wanted a leader, which they wouldn't recognize if it hit them square between the eyes. Effective programming sells itself and trying to market one's way out of a deficit is a recipe for disaster. And two of the three panelists couldn't give a good goddamn about the people of Birmingham, evidenced by the 7 foot fence around their college. Fuck them.

The sad fact is that in Birmingham, among its so-called leaders, mediocrity is the status quo.

It's hard to overstate what a shock it was to my system not getting an academic job. I had sort of jettisoned my redneck identity in favor of "dissident bourgeoisie" and even told people that was what I was. I wracked my brain as to why people wouldn't hire me, but it became clear when I applied for my retiring mentor Conner Bailey's job at Auburn. Conner called me and told me, in so many words, that I was too much of an activist and things became clear. The fact is that there is no place for a redneck antiracist autonomist in academia. As a white man, my lane was to write theory, not be an activist, and the unfortunate fact of the neoliberal multiculturalism of academia is that there have been lanes created (and often shuttered at tenure review) for activist scholars of all types EXCEPT working class ones, and, why would neoliberal multicultural academia create a lane that would be responsible for its ultimate destruction. There are Marxist programs where most of the professors sit in armchairs and write theory, but there are no programs dedicated to the investigation of working class identity and its intersections. There's no departments of Redneck Studies or even working class studies.

Everyone told me it was about fit. I didn't fit anywhere. You can take the redneck out of the trailer park, but you can't take the trailer park out of the redneck. There was no place for me. Robyn and I, who I married in 2013, were dead broke and living with my parents. Robyn had worked for a couple of years as development director for Urban Ministry, which she hated, and then got a great job with Alabama Arise, a state wide policy organization for the poor. She was now a community organizer like me and our life was full of politics and organizing strategy and trying to fuck

stuff up. Some people have called us the power couple, but I don't

necessarily think that, but I do think Robyn should run for office and

eventually governor (she might have to divorce me first). She's such

an amazing woman and, unlike me, universally respected. I'm sure

folks wonder why she's married to me, but I'm real entertaining.

In the Spring of 2015, I was awarded a Greensboro Justice

Fellowship with Highlander Research and Education Center. The

fellowship was a small stipend, travel money to and from

Highlander, and some one-on-one time with other fellows and

Highlander staff and leadership. My cohort was Rocio, DJ, Holden,

Marcelle, and me. I loved spending time with them and talking

about our organizations and they also revealed to me the most

important mistake in creating MCAP. It was patriarchal. This was

its fatal flaw and a big reason why it failed after I left. Patriarchy

and cooperative culture cannot coincide. One patriarch can make the

entire organization about themselves because cooperative people

think about others while patriarchs think about themselves.

Patriarchs drain all the energy out of a cooperative culture. I

sincerely believe that women are better suited for cooperatives because they are socialized to think about others over themselves, while men are taught to assert themselves. As far as mistakes go, this was a doozy because it's difficult to change something as drastically as MCAP needed to change mid-stream.

I also felt a little out of place at Highlander. Most of the attendees at events that Highlander hosts are graduate students, faculty, or other people with privilege. There are very, very few working class people and no rednecks. I think this is a function of the left abandoning working class politics in favor of neoliberal multiculturalism and I'm sure folks there were as suspicious about me as I was about them. Don't get me wrong, I love Highlander; it is my spiritual home, but there needs to be a more developed class consciousness. My latest visit saw the beginnings of that class consciousness and folks were talking seriously about class even if they didn't technically fit the definition of working class.

I was drinking a lot, 6-10 beers a night and my mental health was deteriorating. By this time, our organization was getting pretty well known and I was associated with it. One of the big reasons why I resigned was because we were cast as a white organization because of my leadership, even though we were majority black. We also didn't act like a white organization and just give shit away, so people had no idea what to do with us. I had become sort of a race firebrand and was recognized at many public events. None of this was good for my mental health.

We decided to capitalize on the renewed interest in race created by BLM-Birmingham and hosted a panel called "What Can White People Do About Racism?" The intent was to have a conversation with white people about who we are and how white supremacy shapes us and what we can do to fight it. The panel included Avee-Ashanti Shabazz and my local mentor Jennifer Sanders, who had helped me get over my SJW stage, and others. The openings were great, with ten minute talks from all the panelists. It was well-attended, standing room only, but the discussion got derailed by both black and white elders who didn't understand what we were doing.

The first audience commenter, a veteran black activist, talked for fifteen minutes about anything but what white people can do, and a barrage of other elders recited the same narrative that has been recited in Birmingham for the past 50 years. It was just a conversation about how terrible racism is, which we all knew - that's why we were there - and there was no space for white people to explore their own whiteness collectively and how white supremacy shapes us individually. There was a lot of hub-bub in progressive circles about it, which I guess was good, but to me, it was an utter failure.

The second such panel was put together by Over-the-Mountain Democrats and it was held at a church in Irondale. Avee was supposed to be on the panel but he put a new team member on the panel, Shirah. Again, the talks were great, but the first to the mic after the talks was Avee, who went on a ten minute long rant about separation and the entire discussion was about separation and integration. As I was sitting there listening to the discussion, I was thinking, "why are we still talking about this, there has never been integration because people have to be economically equal to integrate." I tried to say something like this, and about a year later, a middle class black woman would not even look at me because she said that I was for "separation."

By this point, every event that I went to everyone knew me, but people were very distant when they spoke to me. I was drinking copiously and my mental health was deteriorating.

The third panel on race within the span of four months was at the Birmingham Museum of Art for BMA Speaks. I was not invited to participate in this panel and when I showed up with my wife, I was piss drunk. I was a fucking celebrity at the panel and BLM-Birmingham was beginning to come apart at the seams because of gender, general inability to compromise, and Avee being a complete asshole. This shit was really stressing me out and I was having terrible anxiety and drinking all day every day. I also started smoking weed.

Robyn and I left the panel five minutes in.

In the middle of all this drama, our community organizer struck his girlfriend and we had to fire him.

The Black Lives Matter situation deteriorated to the point that there were two Black Lives Matter organizations, a female one and a male one. One of the sides, I can't remember which one, contacted us and asked us to choose. I drank more.

Finally, I invited the community organizer we had fired over to the house and I drank a fifth of Jack Daniels and got high as a chicken. A week earlier, I had had a panic attack that was more like a seizure and after the community organizer left, I tried to get him back on the MCAP team.

I realized that was an insane thing to do and I checked myself into the psych ward of Brookwood Medical Center. One of the things that I focused on while I was there was something that Majadi, who had become something of a spiritual leader, said to me. He said that I was "at war with my ancestors."

REDNECK

Being in the psychiatric wards are not a whole lot of fun. When I got there, I was put in a windowless room and people asked me every five minutes if I was going to off myself. There were lots of strange people who were clearly having worse days/lives than I was and people tried to console me, but I kept thinking that it was prison. I was really scared that I would never be functional again, but I did manage to strike up a friendship with some of the people that I was in there with. We basically did a bunch of stupid therapeutic classes with some nice facilitators and some not so nice facilitators. Two days in, I was a leader and helping people cope with some of their problems. The techs and nurses were great as were most of the patients, but my doctor was the worst.

My doctor showed up at 6:30 am every day and peppered me with questions, but every time I asked her a question, she acted like I was a pain in the ass. She looked at me like I was a science experiment, and if I was, she was a terrible scientist. She immediately took me off Risperdal and put me on Seroquel, which puzzled my mother-in-law, who is a psychiatric social worker.

Going off Risperdal cold turkey is not a very good idea for anyone with the psychotic tendencies that I have. My primary psychiatrist never returned a single call after I went into the hospital and I'm not even sure that he is still alive.

I managed to hold it together long enough to get discharged, but the truth of the matter is that I was worse after the hospital than going in. The only thing that got me through the hospital was thinking about my wife and thinking about the work that we were doing, if somewhat delusionally.

I had been dead to news for the whole week and one of the first articles that I read after I got out of the hospital was that BLM-Birmingham split into BLM-Magic City and BLM-Birmingham, a male and a female group, which shot my stress level through the roof. I deleted both groups from my Facebook friends and tried to watch the Auburn football game, but I was obsessing over all of this stuff and my stress was increasing. I had another panic attack that night after obsessing over the thought that I was broken.

This continued for a couple of days and I was on the verge of despair and was definitely suicidal. Finally, I took some of my left over Risperdal and got to sleep. The Risperdal is key to my functioning. The Seroquel is great for anxiety once your body adjusts to it, but Risperdal keeps my brain in one piece. However, a lot of the damage was done. Once you have real, dangerous suicidal thoughts, it doesn't just leave immediately once you balance out. I had minor panic attacks for the next few weeks and I even had a number of plans about how to off myself that I was afraid to tell anyone about because I didn't want to go back to the hospital. The only good thing about the hospital was that I got on Seroquel and stopped drinking copiously.

And since I didn't have insurance, the whole ordeal, which made me worse, cost me about $10,000.

I did start thinking about what Majadi said to me about my ancestors, being at war with them. In African spirituality, our ancestors are who we are, and, for me, my father's brutality, but in the larger picture, the brutality of rednecks and redneck culture were a source of self-hate for me. My people largely made up the Klan and did most of the lynching and murder, and while my people received little benefit from the racial order, we enforced it with brutality. I hated my people for it and I hated myself for it.

I realized that a great deal of my antiracist work stemmed from this place of self-hate not only for what we did, but also for how we are treated and perceived for what we did. A great deal of why our racial strategy didn't work was because I did it not out of a place of love for my people rednecks, for a desire for us to be better and reach our potential, but a desire to try to erase our history and who we are and were. What I had done was destructive and wrong, and I needed to rethink how I was going to talk about race, and how I was going to talk about it to my people, and if people didn't like it, they could go to hell. I was going to start loving myself and loving my people even if everyone else on Earth told us that we were shit. What I did was cowardly, and, racially speaking, it was time to show real courage - to be the Mad Redneck.

The traditional antiracist strategy is Manichean. It's about casting anyone without perfect racial politics as evil and about prescribing a highly sophisticated, if somewhat ridiculous, racial politics as the only correct way to engage with race. The person who has played a heavy role in popularizing this is Tim Wise, a well-paid provocateur who spends much of his time in the media and on social media demeaning all sorts of people who he sees as his enemy. I respected and mimicked Wise for many years and even emulated some of his tactics, but, while I think race soft-talk is destructive, I also believe that the other pole is counter-productive. Most people don't spend their lives learning the complex and at some points inconsistent anti-racist culture that worries more about who should talk when than what is being said, and while I certainly do think that white people need to learn to shut up and shut up often, I think a culture that prescribes who can talk and what they can say removes the chance for novelty and creativity in addressing race.

Current antiracist theory and practice is more like a religion than an actual approach to getting people where they need to go. It requires unquestioned commitment to a certain dogma, sin, and a great deal of shame. It is not unlike The Church of Christ and my fundamentalist upbringing, and like that upbringing, the social function is to make sense of a an inherently complex and confusing world. Dogma and religion are highly appealing to someone or some people who have suffered, but it, in fact, doesn't change the suffering. It just erects more barriers to genuine human experience, which is what I think that I always have and always will look for. To say, "I don't know what the future holds and I don't have all that many answers" is brutally terrifying especially to people who have suffered, who want a plan for the suffering to stop. Life is suffering, for some more than others. But, the appeal of all forms of dogma, be it white nationalism, antiracism, Leninism, science, or Christianity is that it will end the suffering. It won't. Each other is all we have and probably all we ever will or ever have had.

The first time that I broke down, it took me six months or more to recover because I didn't work to rewire my brain. This time would be different. My uncle offered to teach me how to play the banjo, which doubled as a way to reconnect with my working class past and culture that I shunned and hated. The crazy thing is that, while I started a consultancy a couple of months back called Revolutionary Solutions that had one client, MCAP, I actually was working class again. I was delivering papers for Weld and in 2016 would start driving for Uber. It was a return to who I was, but armed with what seemed to be a lifetime of experience and probably too much theory.

My uncle Carroll helps me with Confessions of a Mad Redneck, a vlog I started during my recovery. He's teaching me how to play the banjo and he plays the background music on the vlog. I love him. He came to my rescue when I first was diagnosed with bipolar by helping me create a garden and he taught me how to play the banjo as a way to recover. He's family. But, he doesn't have perfect, whatever that means, racial politics. He doesn't like Black Lives Matter because he has a son who is police officer and we always have long discussions after the vlog. If he heard Tim Wise, he would turn off immediately, but in our relationship in which we are learning from each other, he is open to discussion and understanding things a different way. I speak on our culture because I love it and the way that I speak on our culture gives me license to criticize it. People, including Carroll, can see that I do it out of love. I don't know what motivates Wise, but it's not love.

I also became more interested in economic solutions, which was always the backdrop for everything that we did - the attempt to change public opinion in a way that would make space for alternatives, specifically the cooperative economy. In 2016, Susan and Majadi would take the mantle of creating a community land trust in Smithfield, the first plank in our strategic plan. "Cooperatives" started popping up all over the city even though they were more cooperating than cooperatives.

I was also developing a relationship with Highlander Research and Education Center to create regional networks for our coalition, which was growing. My Greensboro Justice Fund fellowship gave me pretty exclusive and solid access to Highlander. I love Highlander a lot, as much for what it was as what it is, but I felt some kind of way that there were never any rednecks at any of the meetings that I attended, when the organization was founded to help rednecks, but the way Highlander has evolved, its intersectionality culture runs aground when having to deal with populism. I also love Highlander's focus on art, which was an inspiration for my vlog, Confessions of a Mad Redneck.

The first entry in the Confessions of a Mad Redneck vlog was about the banjo. The banjo was originally an African instrument that got adopted by Appalachian folks. I discussed how the banjo would not exist without slavery and how the banjo, like everything Southern, is beautiful, yet just beneath its surface is madness, the madness of slavery and white supremacy.

My antiracism had changed. Instead of targeting white liberals, who I have little in common with, I decided to try to work with my own people, even if it was virtually. I wanted to cast antiracism as in the self-interest of rednecks, instead of moralizing about us and demeaning us, which we get enough of. I wanted to tell rednecks that our racism and bigotry is hurting us because we are also oppressed, yet we see ourselves as temporarily embarrassed millionaires and that forming a real alliance with other working class folks would go a long way to getting our freedom and independence. I also think this alliance should be based on mutual self-interest and not ideological purity.

At this point, our movement had grown to include Revolutionary Solutions, a government and non-profit consultancy, MCAP, Smithfield Community Action Team, a neighborhood group, Dynamite Hill-Smithfield Community Land Trust, and A Committee of Fools, an activist public theatre group. A Committee of Fools grew out of my observation of BLM-Birmingham and other activism across the country. It seemed to me that social media changed what effective activism was and I saw how unplanned, but sensational activism could garner large amounts of public attention. I had an idea about an action at the Regions Field that would be sensational, yet poignant.

The idea of The Free State of Shuttlesworth was hatched in a conversation between Rob Burton, Berkeley grad student CNE Corbin, and me. The idea was to do an action claiming independence for the 7th Congressional District from Alabama.

A little background: Activist groups in Alabama tried for years to reform the constitution and get home rule for counties and municipalities. As it stands, municipalities can do little without the approval of the state government, which is controlled by conservatives, and this led to many activists stating that "Birmingham has an Alabama problem." Local activists led by Le'Darius Hilliard, Joe Keffer, Doug Hoffman, Mark Myles, and others won a minimum wage increase in Birmingham, the first of its kind in the South, which was subsequently nullified by the State. The activists planned to get minimum wage increase at the state level, which would have been impossible, but instead went forward with an urban strategy on my advice. I gave this strategy to Joe Keffer while smoking a cigarette on Good People Brewing Company's porch at a fundraiser. Although the minimum wage ordinance was nullified, it did inflame the tensions between the state and Birmingham, which was good.

A Committee of Fools sought to further inflame this tension by declaring independence in a sensational, weird, and funny protest that was narrated and live streamed on Facebook. The action reached 5500 people which is amazing for a page with 95 likes. Three days prior to the action, the NAACP filed a 14th Amendment lawsuit about the minimum wage hikes, which we played up the need for independence. The action was fun for everyone involved, got a lot of attention and pretty hilarious and creepy.

At the beginning of summer 2016, I was fairly well known especially in grassroots circles. Public opinion turned sharply against gentrification and REV Birmingham, aided by articles in Kelly's Weld about REV's rather dubious business and communication practices. I told Kelly some three years earlier that he needed to investigate REV after the debacle with PHI. People across the region were becoming interested in the new economy and small investors were popping up for aquaponics. In spite of our and my mistakes and misguided campaigns, we were winning in the realm of public opinion. The mayor was consistently under fire and the council was split between "neighborhood councilors" and mayor-backing councilors. The mayor looked profoundly vulnerable in the

2017 election and forces were coalescing to turn this election into, at least a change election, but more probably, a movement election. There was and still is an opportunity to do something in Birmingham that no one anywhere has done and that's to slow or stop the forces of gentrification and to establish a territorialized new economy even if in a very small way.

In early summer of 2016, we were visited by Gus Newport, a consultant for Grounded Solutions, LLC, who was also the former Executive Director of Dudley Street Neighborhood Initiative, probably the most successful community development project in the nation. He came to work with Dynamite Hill-Smithfield Community Land Trust and its founders and my close friends Susan and Majadi, but wasn't too familiar with Southern organizing. He is friends with Scott Douglas of Greater Birmingham Ministries, and I'm pretty sure Scott told Gus that we do Alinskyan organizing, which we don't. Alinskyan organizing is highly confrontational and sensational organizing. We mostly do popular education, maybe with a splash of Alinskyan sensationalism from time to time. GBM has a reputation of competitiveness with other progressive organizations and they can be difficult to deal with.

Newport was not impressed with us at all, but he didn't understand Southern organizing that well. He kept saying that we needed to get large institutions like the universities to help, but we all know that universities and other institutions don't care about making changes within the city. It's probably the most non-responsive institutional network in the entire country and undoubtedly rivals some third world cities.

The argument for getting universities to help resonated with me. I had always wanted to create a college in Birmingham, but I planned on doing it in maybe twelve years, when I was fifty. Our consultancy, Revolutionary Solutions, had become a cooperative consultancy with about six members, but we weren't getting contracts because nobody had the money to hire us as consultants. We began discussing having classes instead of trying to get contracts, and after a brief conversation in July, the team decided that we were going to create a first-of-its-kind, fully cooperative college called The Cooperative New School for Urban Studies and Environmental Justice. Our team included Susan, Corbin from Berkeley, Karen, a local business whiz, Felicia, a lawyer, and Heather, from U of Florida.

Unfortunately, about this time, MCAP failed. The reasons are complex, but the main reason is that I failed to take feminism seriously when culture-building in the organization. Cooperative cultures cannot survive even one patriarch on the team because women are socialized to put the team before self-interest while men are socialized to put our self-interest above the team. When patriarchs assert their self-interest in a team environment, women and feminists respond not by challenging those patriarchs, but by trying to make accommodations for them. The self-interest of the patriarch then becomes the focus of the team instead of the group as a whole. It has the effect of sucking all the air out of the organization, particularly if it's consensus based. Women and feminist men/non-binary people are best suited for cooperative culture and patriarchal team members should be avoided.

The Cooperative New School is highly diverse. It's wholly owned by the faculty, students, and staff. The purpose is to train the next generation of community organizers, activists, and social entrepreneurs, and we incorporated a non-profit parent company, GroCoop, that is funded out of the Cooperative New School's revenue. GroCoop will provide technical and financial assistance to cooperatives from around the world, but particularly to our star students. It will cost less than community college and students will have an integral part in the management of the cooperative, even having seats on the board.

We held our first event, Economic Futures: Alternatives to Gentrification, in early August of 2016 and got some coverage from the local media. The panel was really great and somewhat surprising for the attendees. We brought in Samir Hazboun from Highlander to sit on the panel and they brought a global perspective to it. There was little grandstanding and a robust dialogue about where we go from here. We even had a mayoral candidate, Randall Woodfin. From that event we began recruiting for our classes, which we called "The Social Movement Bootcamp," and held the first bootcamp class in early September.

A clear strategy was starting to coalesce. Richard, President of MCAP, was working with Avee to create the Grassroots Coalition, which was going to try to replace every major political leader in Birmingham and further the cooperative development of The Cooperative New School and Dynamite Hill-Smithfield Community Land Trust. The development of this strategy paralleled the regional and national strategy of a two front battle over elected officials and cooperative development. Much discussion was happening at Highlander and within the movement, more generally, about how we govern ourselves and how we move from protest to power and self governance.

My wife was still working with Arise and a damn fine organizer in her own right. We're blessed to have, more or less, enough money to live and to be able to work on projects that we are passionate about. Our days are filled with discussion of important issues and just a little shade throwing on other organizers. I'm still making a little money from The Cooperative New School, so things are getting a little easier. I've never been that good at making money, and Robyn is exceedingly patient with me, her dependent. But, we know people all over the South, good people, who work hard and genuinely care. Working in Birmingham and Alabama takes its toll on people. More than a few non-Southern activists and organizers, in fact almost all of them come to the South with grand plans, end up completely lost and discouraged, and leave two years later. Having another person to commiserate with keeps me afloat, even if we love to argue about strategy and tactics.

Shortly after releasing the MCAP Strategic Plan in 2015, a young district attorney and president of the Birmingham Board of Education, Randall Woodfin, approached us about potentially supporting his 2017 mayoral campaign. The meeting was set up by Mark Kelly, a local liberal newspaperman and genuinely good guy who would hook his wagon to Woodfin.

I worked for Kelly at his newspaper, Weld for Birmingham, as a delivery driver for about three years until the newspaper folded. The paper was pretty unique in Birmingham. They had a strong editorial stance, they ran series on gentrification and poverty in Birmingham, and even went far out on a limb to critique the main development non-profit, REV Birmingham, in their dealings with the people of Birmingham. It's really sad that it ultimately folded because it provided such a strong service to the Birmingham community, a voice from the left in Birmingham, advocating for justice and change. I published two editorials in the paper, one on gentrification and one on asset based community development, and Weld allowed a number of community members to publish editorials in the paper. I'm happy that I got to contribute to Weld in my own little way and disappointed that it folded. It seems that the days of small, local papers with strong editorial stances are gone and all that's left is fluff articles and click bait.

Randall ran a great campaign. Let me say that from the beginning. He knocked on doors, he reached out to many different communities in Birmingham, he was organized, and he executed the plan. He came out of nowhere to win an election that everyone thought the incumbent, William Bell, would win in a walk. He networked nationally and raised money almost solely through small donations. He also used the movement community to get elected and turned on us less than two months after inauguration. He began with our community in 2015.

Randall read our plan and seemed high if non- committal on the projects. During the meeting he was open, asked questions, and asked how he could help. He has a weird sort of everyman charisma where he never claims to be an expert, but appears to be listening and engaging with the community. We never thought he was a revolutionary, but we did think that he would listen and that he would work with us.

I met with him a number of times. I told him that if he wanted to get elected that he needed to adopt our plan and that he needed to use social media to stay in the traditional media like Trump. My thoughts were that since he would be at a monetary disadvantage to Bell, he could use free media to leverage the narrative.

He seemed attentive, but there were red flags. He talked shit about Avee Shabazz calling him a sovereign citizen. It's something that I should have caught. He was playing members of the movement off each other, implying that he was going to go with us and not with Shabazz and his team. I missed it completely. I wanted to believe in Randall probably too much and was blinded by the thought of getting a mayor favorable to us. Randall is probably the greatest mistake that I ever made in movement work and it was a big one.

I met with Randall six or seven times leading up to and during the election. We also regularly exchanged text messages. He also showed me a tweet from Chokwe Lumumba, radical mayor of Jackson, Mississippi, that showed Lumumba's support for Randall. Randall of course knew that I admired Lumumba and the work being done in Jackson. I told Randall that if he wanted to be like him Lumumba, he had to support cooperatives. And Randall did.

In August of 2017, Randall endorsed The Black Agenda, a document created by The Grassroots Coalition-Birmingham, a 501c4 organization that grew out of the MCAP Strategic Plan. The plan was wide ranging and included policing reform, cooperative economics, and transportation. Randall carefully guided the debate about economics toward black-owned businesses and community land trusts. It was an explicit endorsement of one type of cooperative institution, community land trusts, and an implicit endorsement of cooperatives generally. Randall had previously put participatory budgeting and citizens oversight of police in his platform, after which I personally endorsed him. After endorsing The Black Agenda, The Cooperative New School endorsed Randall.

Bell hired Matrix, a political consulting firm, to attack Randall. Matrix and the Bell campaign paid a number of grassroots organizers to switch sides. I do not know if or how much they were paid, but they did switch sides in the middle of the election. By switch sides, I mean, they struggled with us against Bell's gentrification and militarized policing agenda for years and when it came time to kick his ass out, they joined him. One activist's switch drove a wedge in Black Lives Matter-Birmingham of which they were one of the founding members. In retrospect, it would have probably made more sense to just take the money because the name of the person in political office ultimately doesn't matter because the Big Mules always have and still do control Birmingham. In a city and state this corrupt, there's little room for idealism and a mercenary attitude is rewarded institutionally.

The Bell campaign also recruited a number of online influencers to attack Randall, and the arguments online reached a fever pitch in the months leading up to the election.

But none of it phased Randall. He had an army of free social media personalities to fight for him because they believed in him, and nothing Matrix or Bell could do would stick. Randall's staff also seemed quite a bit more adept at using social media than the Bell campaign, creating humorous memes and driving the narrative. Randall won in a landslide.

Randall's first move was to create transition committees that brought together people from all sectors of Birmingham to supposedly craft his agenda. There was a social justice committee, which many movement folks were on. It seemed like we were gaining institutional legitimacy, but I chose not to be on the committees because I wanted to maintain my independence. Some people were raising red flags.

We were in the process of creating the Cooperative Business Development Center with a couple of black women organizers and a radicalized former small business owner, which was to be an incubator for cooperative businesses. The center was gaining some traction. We were working with the Woodlawn Foundation to create a cooperative grocery store and we were working with a number of other people to create cooperatives. People openly wondered how much of Randall's promises he was actually going to do and some members of the CBDC were quite skeptical of all Randall's initiatives.

The transition committee process included a number of public meetings to craft a social justice agenda for this city. This included an Office of Social Justice. There was a wide range of recommendations ranging from pollution to cooperatives and everything in between.

But, things began to fall apart for Randall not long into his tenure. In January of 2018, Randall announced that the city was going to build a stadium. It was the first thing he did in spite of the fact that he had said during the campaign that it was not a priority. The cost was $90 million over 30 years and the stadium would be owned by the Birmingham Jefferson Civic Center, which is essentially a white shadow government, and not the city. Randall touted unrealistic returns on the stadium for the city, numbers which included the redevelopment of Caraway Hospital, a project which would only be taken on by an insane person or someone with a healthy subsidy. I challenged Randall on it on Facebook. He responded that he wanted to talk.

I spoke with him by phone. I told him that I'd get behind it if he got a community benefits agreement on the stadium. He agreed. I wrote a plan to include CBA benefits in the bidding process. Randall agreed in writing to get a CBA in a response to City Councilor Darrell O'Quinn's written set of questions. I even chewed out O'Quinn at a community meeting in front of about thirty people. This was not what we voted for.

There was never a CBA. Randall's progressive/movement support began to disintegrate. I still believed in him, but some of the things that were red flags, like his business community support, began to pop up in my mind. Every movement person was waiting on the transition committee process to see if it was all real or fake.

Randall reserved the Alabama Theatre and gave the results of the transition committee process. It was vague and indeterminant, but one thing was clear. Randall was a neoliberal reformer. Randall was going to take the city from an essentially Third World banana republic to a modern neoliberal city where gentrification was king and businesses could make tons of money. He did promise to create an Office of Social Justice, but that has not yet happened. People were very disappointed.

The final straw and the moment that completely dissolved Randall's credibility was when he refused to make Birmingham a Sanctuary City, which he promised to do during the campaign. Randall had failed to do anything that he promised to the movement; not one thing. I don't know if this is because Randall is incompetent in terms of moving a bureaucracy or if it is because he never really intended to do it in the first place. Either way it makes him a liar.

Birmingham is perpetually missing its potential. There was a moment, one moment, when everything seemed to come together. I don't like big crowds at all, but I decided to go to the celebration of

Randall's victory on the night of the election. The people there were what Birmingham really is and what it could be. Avee Shabazz, Mark Kelly, Michael Hansen, Julia Juarez, Martez Files, and many many others. The campaign had brought these people together in a way that Birmingham had never seen before and it was truly powerful. The people there could have supported and fought for Randall as he tried to do something no one else has ever done anywhere. But, that moment is gone and the opportunity is missed. The lesson learned is that white suburban capitalists control Birmingham and have since 1871 including during and after the Civil Rights Movement.

Big Mule, or Alabama capitalist usually living in the Birmingham suburbs, Sid Smyer famously said, "I'm a segregationist but I'm not a damn fool." The Big Mules could see that holding on to segregation was going to destroy their power, and they eliminated it and reorganized the government in order to maintain that power. Birmingham was a colony of the Big Mules under direct rule during Jim Crow. Now it is a colony under indirect rule.

I moved to Montgomery because my wife is now the executive director of Alabama Arise. My work in Birmingham is over and most of my activism is both a hobby and national/international. I'm semi-retired from activism, working at a shop, and restoring my 1985 Toyota 4Runner. It's been a difficult transition. It's not often that something that you feel is your life's work like Birmingham just abruptly ends and you're left with an unknown and open future. I don't know what is in store for me, but I do know that I'm proud of the work we did together in Birmingham. We came damn close, damn close to achieving something truly revolutionary and I hope history remembers all of us for that. It's proof that it is possible, even in the South.

In my journey, I have begun to grasp what being a redneck means. It means recognizing the wisdom and the folly of our ancestors. It means pride of work and working hard for its own sake, because it's spiritually healing. It means commitment to family, kin and chosen. It means patience. It means sharing openly with younger people and listening, not uncritically, to elders. It means supporting and loving the people around you before taking a plate for yourself. The term redneck was popularized during the

West Virginia Mine Wars of 1912-1921 in indicates solidarity. Rednecks wore red neckerchiefs to symbolize their solidarity and it wasn't just white people. It literally means taking care of those struggling with you.

All this stuff is there in redneck culture along with white supremacy and misogyny. The key is to accentuate the positive and eliminate the negative; to work on self so that we can better serve and help others. It means servant leadership.

Ultimately, though, there's no place for rednecks in academia and activism. We're too loud, too white, too male, too much. Academia is full of people whose self-worth is wrapped up in being the smartest person in the room and that kind of conceit is actively penalized by rednecks.

We're the workers. We work quietly and proudly, we take care of our community and families, we well up with pride listening to "Roll On" by Alabama, we feel validated by "A Country Boy Can Survive" by Hank Williams, Jr, and are justified by "Long Haired Country Boy" by Charlie Daniels. As Vanity Fair said, you can never escape who society says you are. I'm back to fixing cars, working with my hands as well as my head.

And yes, it all sounds great on the surface and we get a ton of shit wrong, but there is still value in who we are and what we do in spite of how it's fucked up and, in my case, the fucked up way I got here. I'm back to where I started, on the auto shop floor, with maybe a little more wisdom and a lot more experience. My future is an open question, but I'm happy here and working with a pride and sense of purpose that I never did as a young man.

MOVEMENT

Everything in life is about movement. The blood cells in our body move around carrying oxygen from our breath. We dance, we make love. We grow and change, evolve and revolt. We cross through open territory and we destroy closed ones by our presence and actions there. This memoir is loosely based on Deleuze and Guattari's ideas of deterritorialization, reterritorialization and lines of flight. But, mostly, it's about freedom - about the right to grow and change as individuals and as communities. The right to move from one identity to the next and the right to leave when the space becomes striated.

Deterritorialization simply means to destroy, to remove structures, to make space smooth. It's how the power of the multitude, a singularity of infinitely diverse people and communities, is used to flatten the Earth through labor, material or immaterial. For years, the multitude has deterritorialized everything it touches. It has destroyed oppressive structures, changed policy, and revolted against the powerful. It has said "ya basta" over and over and over, but at this point in history, the multitude must exercise its reterritorializing power of decentralized self-governance.

The power begins with individuals becoming "woke." In an individual's relationship with movement, we are forced to deterritorialize ourselves. [The young white supremacist that I was began this deterritorializing process by listening to hip hop and Rage Against the Machine.] At that moment, my relationship with movement began and the process of deterritorialization was put into play. Deterritorialization and reterritorialization are not unidirectional, but consist of ebbs and flows, of forwards and back, like a dance, like making love. Thus, the act of deterritorializing the white supremacist was an act of profound love, not only of myself, but of the world around me. It was a dividing cell of self love, an attempt to better connect with the world around me, and something done quite unconsciously.

The relationship to movement is a process of learning and unlearning and exploration. It is a relationship to life and living beings and to the primordial ooze that brought us here, our first ancestor. We are nomads. The majority of human history was spent wandering in the wilderness looking for food and processing always novel information. Yet, sedentary agriculture became a n

and it is hard to imagine a nomadic life now. Yet, we can.

Hakim Bey came up with the concept of ontological anarchy, which

I don't particularly understand, but to me it is the truth that there are

many truths. Such modern nomadism is not so much of a movement

physically, but to experience the different material, intellectual, and

spiritual truths and to experience as many of these truths as possible.

This leads to no answers, only exponentially more questions, more

deterritorializing and reterritorializing to the point that change is not

only inevitable, but constant and quickening in speed. A singularity

has an almost infinite speed.

At some point, this quickening ceases to be revolution and

begins to be evolution. Once the structures and spaces and territories

that bind us are removed, human evolution proceeds at a breakneck

pace. Utopia is achieved not because everything is perfect, but

because nothing is ever the same. Who we are today is not expected

to be the us of tomorrow or of yesteryear. We use our individual and

collective histories to manifest new and novel histories on a daily,

even hourly basis. There is no return to the past; there couldn't be

because no one knows what the past really is. Like all reality, the past is made in the present and reflects present conditions. This is

not to say to forget the ancestors, but to understand that the ancestors

want us to create an new future, not their past.

To set this process in motion, to bring a relationship between

communities and individuals and movement, we must have an

understanding of the past and present that enable the new future. My

analysis was of Birmingham, but the method will be broadly

applicable to any city.

Many urban scholars, including Neil Brenner, are arguing that

urbanization as a global process has no outside. I agree with this

assessment. Brenner, Ignacio Farias and others have argued that

cities are not a thing, but a process; othersactor-network theorists see

more opportunity in cities than afforded by spatial theorists like

Brenner. To me, they are both right - urbanization is a process of

territorializing urban assemblages and networks. Specifically,

urbanization is the process of territorializing the protocols that give a

network consistency, facilitate communication, and provide

durability. This point of view recognizes both the durability and the

point-of-change within the urbanization process. The points-of-change are weak points within territorialized protocols that can be exploited. Movements are looking for the exploit.

NETWORKS

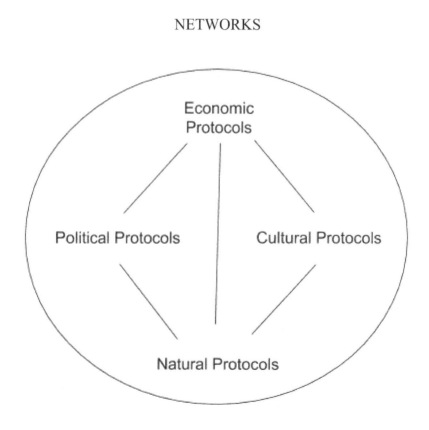

Protocols are institutional behaviors that allow networks of organizations, institutions, and individuals to transmit information within the network with consistency and durability. These networks are simultaneously political, economic, cultural, and natural. For instance, a water system in a city has water (natural), infrastructure to move and clean water (political and natural), expectations that each citizen can go to the tap and get clean water (cultural), and money from taxation to build and maintain the system (economic and political). The same can be said for policing services, land use planning, transportation, education, and capital and job creation. The consistency of these protocols is what makes the network work. Disrupting these protocols is one way to create the conditions for change.

TERRITORIAL STATE SYSTEM

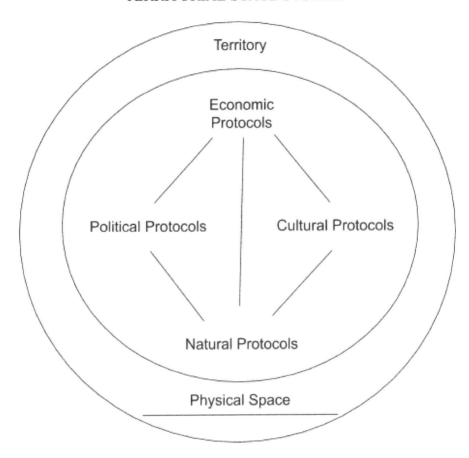

When a set of protocols is institutionally connected to a physical space, a territorial state system is created. The power of the state is a derivative of its ability to use protocols to control physical space or territory. Many protesters have taken to blocking freeways as a form of protest. This directly undermines the territorial integrity of the local territorial state system, which includes all sets of institutions involved including healthcare, education, corporations, media, and so on. This undermining of the territorial integrity of the state stretches the state system, which makes reforms easier to achieve. The state gives reforms as an attempt to reestablish territorial control, though with the state in a changed position.

Traditionally, the state has used reforms or repression to quell social movements, usually a combination of both. Thus, the goal of deterritorializing powers should be to force reforms, and, while all too often, reformers do not push for the goals of protestors, it does create a reterritorializing process of the state with a changed set of protocols.

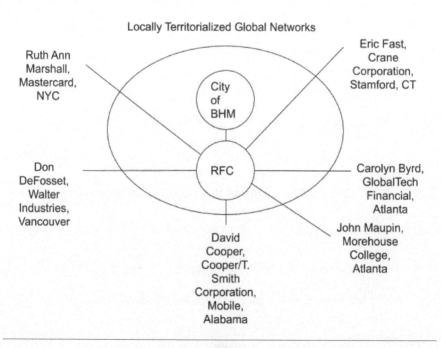

This is an example of the territorial state system in Birmingham. The top, inner circle represents the actual state, Birmingham city government, while the bottom inner circle is a representation of Regions Bank. The city needs Regions to govern because Regions has over 6000 local employees and had $1 billion in income in the first six months of 2016. This is two and a half times the entire budget of the city of Birmingham. Because of this, Birmingham is reliant on Regions to establish the territorial integrity of the state. Regions, other corporations, and other organizations in the growth coalition are part of the state system that must maintain territorial integrity and thus power.

The names outside of the outer circle are names of board members of Regions Financial Corporation. They are far flung from all over the world, which is interesting because Regions is a locally based company. Other organizations like Wells Fargo who are active in Birmingham would have even further flung networks. These networks are territorialized locally even though they are global networks. Transnational corporations are territorialized locally hundreds if not thousands of times throughout the globe and often operate under decentralized management systems that function based on consistent network protocols.

Social movements must recognize clearly that we are fighting against global players who know all too well how to manipulate local politics to their end. It is imperative that we build similar types of networks that can leverage scaled power on local communities. At this point in history, it is virtually impossible for a fully local movement to combat the efforts of transnational corporations. We must be transnational too. Often points of leverage are thought to be found in local politics, but I would posit that no matter who the politicians are in a particular locale, they are still at the behest of transnational corporations because they provide jobs and capital. Building a real, sustainable local economy, a fifty year job, seems like the best option for cutting transnationals out of the equation.

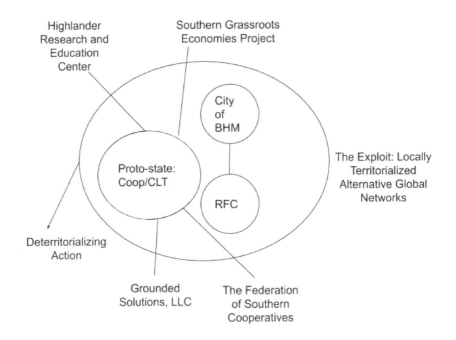

As I said earlier, deterritorializing action creates space for reforms. However, reforms are generally inadequate for more than incremental change, i.e. a shift in protocols. In order to replace protocols completely, we must create alternative institutional situations with different sets of protocols. That institutional situation is the proto-state, or the community land trust/cooperative combo. A community land trust is an institution of territorial control that is decentralized and owned by the community. The hallmark feature of a CLT is dual ownership in which the trust owns the grounds of a piece of property and the individual business or homeowner owns the improvements to the grounds. This creates permanently affordable housing by taking land out of the market and creates an institution of community-based land use planning. A worker owned cooperative is a business owned by the employees.

If you pair the two, you get a structure that mirrors that of the traditional state. You have a territorial entity combined with a set of organizations providing capital and jobs. However, the protocols are profoundly different and, instead of being top down, are characterized as inherently democratic. This proto-state is the exploit that we are looking for.

Engaging in a movement for democratic self-governance is the process of creating new human beings. We are used to banging on the system - of protest, riots, and revolutions - but rarely have we been successful in the process of self governance. While there is still place for deterritorializing action, the reterritorializing process must be taken away from reformers and placed into the hands of revolutionaries. Through this process we must develop the leadership and community skills to actually govern ourselves and to build organizations that will become institutions that can stand on their own, have political power, and do all the things that the current suite of institutions currently don't.

The largest barrier is ideological purity. All too often, committed revolutionaries are more committed to their perceived solution than working out solutions in a community education process. This is true for organizers and activists as diverse as black nationalists, intersectional feminists, and socialists. Many of these folks have been harmed by one system of oppression or another and find solace in "truth" and rigidity, when the answer lies in hammering out consensus within communities and self governance of communities. This requires compromise with people who are different from you and many times, even the smallest difference derails efforts at self-governance. We must not be afraid to implement partial or incomplete plans and work them out through the self-governance process. By doing this, we will be changed from deterritorializing protestors into reterritorializing governors of self.

An example of a proto-state in Birmingham is the collaboration between Dynamite Hill-Smithfield Community Land Trust, SWEET Alabama (a non-profit), and The Cooperative New School (a global cooperative). The land trust controls land, The

CNS controls labor, and SWEET will control capital, the three things you need for a functioning economy.

There will also be many options because many proto-states can exist within a relatively limited geographic areas. This will allow affinity groups to work together and people who don't get along to have options not to work together. I even envision fundamentalist Christian proto-states in which I would not want to live, but they would be free to enact whatever kind of draconian cultures they wish. If people don't like it, they can leave. The only thing that larger state systems would do would be to provide absolute freedom of movement from one place to another so that if someone has no proto-state options in Alabama, they can move to a place where they do.

Engaging in movements is positive and transformative. It has profoundly changed my life. I want to end this memoir by telling a story about why I'm in movements, and my good friend Majadi Baruti.

I met Majadi sometime in 2015 at a protest about the sewer debt in Birmingham. He and I instantly hit it off and didn't really participate in the protest, but just talked about movement stuff. He came over to our house in Five Points and we talked for a number of hours.

Eventually, Majadi started working for MCAP. He and his partner, Susan, were fascinated with our strategic plan for a democratic economy. They decided that they wanted to create a community land trust in Smithfield called Dynamite Hill-Smithfield Community Land Trust to gain independence and combat gentrification. The two of them are some of my favorite people and Majadi is one of my closest friends.

But my friendship with Majadi became something deeper than just the nuts and bolts of movement work. He has helped me to get in touch with my inner Mad Redneck and has become something of a spiritual advisor for me. He helped me to understand, by telling me that I was at war with my ancestors, both my whiteness, my real whiteness, not the one that is told to me by the traditional antiracist line, and he has helped me to understand why and how my people are oppressed. He has helped me to understand why and how I am oppressed because of my culture and helped me not only to deal with my oppression, but to address in a real way what our ancestors did to black people and to process it without succumbing to self-hate.

I hate to speak for Majadi, but from what he has told me, he has gotten in touch with his Southerness and the Southerness that he never knew existed being from the rust belt. His Great-Grandfather was a bluesman and he started to recognize that cultural idioms and food and accent were all rooted in Southern culture. We talk to each other like old Southern friends, like my friends Jason and Bryan, with no pretense and no expectations except to share our life with each other and to support our individual if interconnected struggles.

We have a live vlog that we do called "The Redneck and the Shaman," and our love for and trust of each other comes through to the audience. The last one we did was on The Movement for Black Lives Policy Platform and we had 175 live views which is really incredible.

The reason I move is so that I can have the experience of being a redneck and having brotherly love for a black nationalist from Chicago. "The Redneck and the Shaman" is not something that can happen without movement. I've loved, lost, bled, died, and been reborn many times and only through these movements can the rich life of a revolutionary be led. Peace y'all.

Made in USA - Kendallville, IN
1208410_9781095302576
12.08.2020 0912